Beyond the Ca

Raghunathan is an academic, corporate executive, author, columnist and a hobbyist. He has made Bengaluru his home.

He taught finance at the Indian Institute of Management, Ahmedabad, for a couple of decades before turning a banker as the president of ING Vysya Bank in Bengaluru. He is currently the CEO of the GMR Varalakshmi Foundation. He continues to pursue his academic interests as an adjunct professor at the University of Bocconi in Milan, Italy, and the Schulich School of Business, York University, in Toronto, Canada.

He has been writing extensively for leading newspapers and magazines and currently blogs for the *Times of India*. His many books include *Duryodhana*; *Locks, Mahabharata and Mathematics*; *Ganesha on the Dashboard*; *Corruption Conundrum*; *Don't Sprint the Marathon* and *Games Indians Play*.

Raghu has probably the largest collection of antique locks in the country, has played chess at the all-India level, and was briefly a cartoonist for a national daily.

Veena Prasad writes essays and fiction, creates crosswords and content, for children and adults, makes compost at home, and occasionally writes songs.

Her first book, *Forever Forty*, celebrates the life of Col Vasanth V., an army officer who was awarded the Ashoka Chakra for his gallantry. She also has to her name a book of themed crossword puzzles for children, *Fun Across Zoom Down*.

Her essays are centred around creativity, compassion, science and meaningful education. Her stories, book reviews and crosswords have been published by the *Deccan Herald*, *Hindu*, *Young World*, Pratham Books, *Brainwave*, *Reading Hour*, The Hoot and others.

Beyond the Call of Duty

V. RAGHUNATHAN
AND
VEENA PRASAD

HarperCollins *Publishers* India

First published in India in 2015 by
HarperCollins *Publishers* India

Copyright © V. Raghunathan 2015

Inside illustrations: Vishakha Ramamurthy

P-ISBN: 978-93-5177-264-4
E-ISBN: 978-93-5177-265-1

2 4 6 8 10 9 7 5 3 1

V. Raghunathan and Veena Prasad assert the moral right
to be identified as the authors of this work.

HarperCollins *Publishers*
A-75, Sector 57, Noida, Uttar Pradesh 201301, India
1 London Bridge Street, London, SE1 9GF, United Kingdom
Hazelton Lanes, 55 Avenue Road, Suite 2900, Toronto, Ontario M5R 3L2
and 1995 Markham Road, Scarborough, Ontario M1B 5M8, Canada
25 Ryde Road, Pymble, Sydney, NSW 2073, Australia
195 Broadway, New York, NY 10007, USA

Typeset in 10.5/14.7 Sabon by
R. Ajith Kumar

Printed and bound at
Thomson Press (India) Ltd

Dedication by V. Raghunathan

My good friend Yasaswy, who was the inspiration behind this book.

————

Dedication by Veena Prasad

*To those who live life
Doing their absolute best
Unbound by duty.*

Contents

Preface

THE IDEA OF THIS book originated in 2009, over lunch with a very good friend of mine, the late Shri N.J. Yasaswy – a true man of letters in the highest traditions of scholarship. Two of my books – *Paradoxes and Dilemmas* (Penguin, 2010) and *Don't Sprint the Marathon* (HarperCollins, 2010) – were nearing completion, and he was enquiring about their progress. It was during this conversation that he suggested I consider writing a book on some of the forgotten British gentlemen who were not necessarily administrators during the colonial times but who went way beyond their call of duty to contribute to India.

He thought that it would not only be a worthy tribute to some truly remarkable personalities but would also help to keep their inspiring stories alive and relevant. His argument was that while we are quick to criticize and condemn the British era, there were some remarkable people among them who had made India their karmabhoomi and contributed enormously to pushing the boundaries of knowledge and social reforms in this part of the globe. This sounded like an excellent idea, and I told him so.

However, deep down like most Indians, I have never quite come to terms with the fact that a handful of Britons should have ruled over millions upon millions of us for three centuries. It is difficult to say anything nice about anyone who ruled over one's people, unless one suffers from the Stockholm syndrome. Besides,

I knew very little of such English gentlemen and their specific achievements. Ordinarily, my concurrence with Yasaswy over his excellent suggestion would have gone the way many of our good intentions go.

But those who know Yasaswy (incidentally, he is the one who promoted the Institute of Chartered Financial Analysts of India and the IBS Business School in the country), would also know that he was nothing if not persistent and persuasive. And my wife Meena and I were bound to him and his wife Shobha in an unstated contract of delicious fortnightly lunches, conjured up by Shobha from the forgotten recipes of Andhra Pradesh. The subject was bound to come up again and again, and having accepted that his idea was a truly good one, there was no way I could not act on it, even if I suffer from the standard malady of authors, namely, unless an idea has been burning inside my head for a while, and unless I feel the idea becoming 'my own idea', I cannot start writing.

But I realized that my standard rules wouldn't apply here. In the meanwhile, Yasaswy had already sent me an email suggesting a few names (some of which have found their way into this book) to work on!

Paradoxical as it sounds, the only way to overcome procrastination is to act. So I started looking into some of the names suggested by Yasaswy and others that I encountered on Google. To my pleasant surprise, I found quite a few of them who were not 'rulers' of India in the sense that, say, a Lord Clive, Hastings, Macaulay, Dalhousie, Curzon or Mountbatten were – as a Governor General or a Viceroy – but men who came to work in India as ordinary folk, fell in love with India and Indians, and then went on to contribute to India beyond their call of duty.

Of course, one can question the intent and motive of all the work done by a colonial Briton in India. We can ask: Why are we so West-centred? Why is it necessary to celebrate Englishmen who were our colonizers? The British Raj did us so much harm;

so what is this book trying to do – defend the Raj? Weren't the British trying to advance their own objectives in whatever they did? Is this book trying to build the case that they did it for altruistic purposes? Why these specific men and not some others whom some may consider equally or more deserving? We can quibble on these and many more similar questions and decry the very idea of writing a book that 'eulogizes' the British. To such detractors, I can only say that this book is about those Britons who made India their karmabhoomi even if it wasn't their janmabhoomi.

Coming back to my early days with the book, I feverishly worked on a couple of chapters in the months following our lunch, and I found the idea more and more engaging. But progress was slow for a variety of reasons. For one, this project sounded and came close to being a historical one and I am not a historian by a long shot. The subject needed enormous quantities of reading and trawling through unfamiliar territory. This made for plodding progress. Most books relevant to the project were highly specialized ones and not easily available, unless one was willing to spend months in some sprawling dark library. With a full-time job, this was hardly an option, especially given my determination that I wasn't about to embark on a new career – that of a historian.

I made one important decision, even if it was a decision of convenience – that this book, if and when written, would be based essentially on research material available online. Thanks to the volume of information I was about to find online – with a lot of references and ancient books being available for free – this fortunately became possible.

However, notwithstanding my intent to go firing on all cylinders on this project, my other two books, which were just coming up for publication, demanded a lot of my attention. And following those two books, I started working on another project feverishly (which became *Ganesha on the Dashboard* – Penguin, 2012), with my brother-in-law Dr Eswaran, about the lack of scientific temper in India. Feverishly because Dr Eswaran was in extremely fragile health and did not have long to live (sadly, he passed away two months before the publication of the book). Just as the writing of *Ganesha on the Dashboard* was coming to an end, another of my books that had been incubating inside my head for years started taking shape. This was *Locks, Mahabharata and Mathematics* (HarperCollins, 2013). This was the kind of book that, once begun, would brook no break in the chain of my thoughts until completed.

In the meanwhile, Yasaswy most unexpectedly and tragically passed away towards the end of 2011. And now, call it loyalty towards a departed friend if you will, I simply had to go back to *Beyond the Call of Duty*. Throughout 2012, I had been feeling guilty about not going full steam ahead with the project, and finally it was only in 2013 that I managed to dust the old chapters and dive back in with renewed vigour.

It was around this time that Veena Prasad, my co-author for this book, got in touch with me through my website after reading one of my earlier books, *Games Indians Play* (Penguin, 2006). She shared some of her own writings on similar themes. Finding her sincerity of purpose and quality of writing to be of the highest standard, I spoke to her about *Beyond the Call of Duty* and asked if the idea interested her enough to become my co-author – which it did, and so here we are together on the cover of this book as authors.

From here on, let me speak for both of us. Our writing styles are different, but not very. We have each written five chapters in the book, but we aren't telling you who wrote which, and leave it as a gentle teaser for you to figure out – if you care for such a teaser, that is!

Neither of us is a historian, and we have not arrogated ourselves the role of even amateur historians. We have tried to be mere storytellers and told the stories of a dozen outstanding British gentlemen: all of them from colonial India, except one, Mark

Tully. These were men who loved India and Indians and went way beyond their call of duty when doing *in* India, and *for* India, what they did. They were young men, barely out of their teens, when they came to our country, thousands of miles away from their families, at a time when any two-way correspondence would take several months. They came to a land which had different languages, a different climate, different food, different diseases, different religions, different gods, different attires, different appearances and a different way of life from those they were used to back home.

And yet they devoted virtually their entire lives to issues of relevance mostly to India and Indians, often at the cost of being at loggerheads with their own authorities. What inspired one of them to form the Asiatic Society? Or a junior army doctor to spend his youth peering into the guts of a mosquito? Or another young man to spend years building bridges and dams? Or to devote half a lifetime to decoding the Pali script – a study which would help extend the span of Indian history by centuries? Or to laying railway lines? In many cases, what the gentlemen did was not even part of their job descriptions. Personally, we are in no doubt that their inspiring stories need to be told and retold. And this book is a small effort in that direction.

The book was meant to cover the lesser-known English gentlemen whose stories needed re-telling. But as it usually happens through the evolution of any idea, the final ten chosen by us are not necessarily those who are relatively unknown in India. For example, Mark Tully is quite well known (and he is also the exception, being a contemporary and not from the British Raj). Also well-known is Ronald Ross, a Nobel laureate of malaria fame. And perhaps to a slightly lesser extent, so is Sir Arthur Cotton, who is extremely well-known in certain parts of Andhra Pradesh and Tamil Nadu even today.

And yet, even their stories are rarely told to our youth, and if told, perhaps not often enough to leave an impression. For example, few of our school children are informed of the inspiring lives and achievements of Ross or Arthur Cotton, leave alone those of Mountstuart Elphinstone, James Prinsep, William Jones, W.H. Sleeman, the Cunningham brothers, R.M. Stephenson, John Chapman or Archibald Campbell. Ask a hundred well-educated people if they know who set up the Asiatic Society, and chances are ninety-nine will draw a blank. The same applies to questions such as who were the people principally responsible for laying the foundations of the Indian railway system, or who minimized the menace of the thugee system in India.

And therein lies the need for telling these stories, which, in our view, are stories of sheer human spirit, stories of excellence, perseverance and application, stories that celebrate the satisfaction of a job well done. These are the stories of men for whom recognition was merely a collateral benefit and never the objective.

And now for some aspects relating to the 'research' on the personalities we have covered in this book. As I stated earlier, we neither mean the book to be a historical nor a biographical text about the individuals covered – which in many cases do exist. Our major focus in this book, therefore, has been the contributions of these gentlemen to India. Most of these gentlemen did a lot of work in other countries as well. But we have focused only on their work done in India, mostly for Indians.

Most of these men had extensive families, which remain largely untouched in this book for reasons of focus and relevance. We have done our best to retain the accuracy of the facts, except where our subjective judgment may have been warranted. While we have properly documented the bibliography with the relevant references, the truth is we also went through scores of websites to get meat for our stories. These we have merely listed (with the dates of extraction) as 'websites referred', and not as numbered references as part of the bibliography.

I do hope my friend Yasaswy will be happy with the result, wherever in the heavens he is. And finally, I am also certain that Yasaswy would have entirely agreed with the disclaimer that this book has not been written in praise of the East India Company or the British Raj but of a few individuals, many of whom may have had affiliations with the Company but who were mostly ordinary young men whose inspirational stories may be as relevant today as they were then.

V. Raghunathan

Introduction

The Company, the Raj, the System and Us

IT'S FUNNY WHEN YOU think about it. It was a potato that was responsible for a handful of European countries asserting their dominion over much of the world, India included![1] That, and significant advances in maritime technology and navigational skills that the Portuguese had developed during the seventeenth century.

Intrepid sailors that they were, they set out on voyages that lasted years, with only the kinds of provisions that had long shelf lives but little by way of nutrition. And so, after that path-breaking trip to the Indian shores around the Cape of Good Hope (July 1497- January 1499), Vasco da Gama found that he had lost more than half of his crew to scurvy, a condition that results from a deficiency of Vitamin C. With this kind of mortality, it was unlikely that world domination would be within reach.

As chance would have it, da Gama's colleagues (led by Francisco Pizarro in 1532) happened to reach the shores of South America, where they picked up an unassuming tuber and stashed it away on board, along with other spoils. This one, however, did not spoil. It lasted long enough to provide the sailors with their required dosage of Vitamin C, as a result of which the survival rate became high enough for them to contemplate further journeys. And so the potato made its way to distant lands along with European

1

sailors and has today become the staple export of many countries, including India – where it was not even a native crop to start with! This is just one example of the unexpected ways in which European domination left behind fruits along with scars.

From the Europeans' point of view, this new discovery which made long voyages possible enabled them to exploit the sea route for their spice imports from South Asia (or the East Indies). Hitherto, the spice trade had been essentially land-locked, passing through much of Asia and the Middle East. This involved resorting to intermediaries for prolonged periods, making the imports expensive for the Europeans.

But sea trade, for the first time, permitted them to cut out the intermediaries, and this helped them increase their profits significantly. Spain, a neighbour of Portugal, another maritime power of the time, was not to be left behind for long and joined the fray. Between themselves, they enjoyed a virtual monopoly of the spice trade between Asia and Europe – until the Spanish Armada was defeated by the British in 1588.

This victory over the Spanish Armada enabled some of the London traders who had been struggling to make inroads into the South Asian subcontinent to win trade concessions from the Mughal Empire, leading them to form the East India Company, or more formally, 'Governor and Company of Merchants of London Trading into the East Indies' for the purpose of making profits by importing spices from East Indies, which included Far-Eastern Asia. The company was founded by a royal charter virtually on the last day of 1600.

The first hundred years of the British East India Company remained a difficult period for the company, with its supremacy being challenged by the Dutch. However, with the Mughal licence for trading in hand, 'the company settled down to a trade in cotton and silk piece goods, indigo, and saltpetre, with spices from South

India. It extended its activities to the Persian Gulf, Southeast Asia, and East Asia.'[2]

In the 1690s, another company was established for more or less the same purpose as the original company – each eating into the other's profits – so that the two merged in 1708 as the 'United Company of Merchants of England trading to the East Indies'. This was *the* East India Company from here on.

The company managed its affairs through a board or court of directors. With the sun already setting on the Mughal Empire, the company's settlements were increasingly subject to harassment by the many independent princes, big and small, so that the company started meddling in the local politics more and more. *Encyclopedia Britannica* tells us that the company soon acquired effective control of Bengal Presidency in 1757. This was followed by Madras and Bombay Presidencies in due course, to a point where it effectively managed not merely the commercial, but the political, social and economic affairs of these regions as well.

In effect, the East India Company was a company that owned a nation – India. Its main business had become operating India, with its India policy being shaped through shareholders' meetings. This meant that a policy could be tweaked as desired – by purchasing some stocks with voting rights to increase the weight in favour of that policy. The company over a period of time had assembled a military of its own to ward off foreign competitors like the French East India Company. It also created its own administrative departments to manage the territories under its direction. In effect, the company had become an imperial power in its own right. Moreover, the revenues from the three presidencies, particularly Bengal, were being used for the personal enrichment of the company officials administering the territories.

This often meant that the interests of the British government back home were increasingly being compromised, and it felt compelled to rein in the company's growing power and gain a share of the revenues, especially as the territories the company was beginning to control were beginning to cost the United Kingdom dearly in terms of revenues lost. As a consequence, the Regulating Act (1773), Pitt's India Act (1784) and a series of other charters were passed to help the British government exercise active control over its India administration through a regulatory board that could report to the Parliament. Thus, the British took the first step towards establishing formal political control of India.

However, the company's stranglehold on commercial and political levers controlling India was beginning to slacken by the turn of the nineteenth century, and by 1834 the company was reduced to a managing agency for the British government of India. At the same time, the company's tea trade with China was overshadowing the Indian cotton goods trade. By the turn of the century, the company was paying for Chinese tea with opium exports, much to the distress of the Chinese, which would lead to the First Opium War from 1839 to 1842, and then the second one from 1856 to 1860 – a period that would coincide with the Indian uprising of 1857. Effective 1873, the united East India Company, born in 1708, died as a legal entity.

The result of India's First War of Independence was the passing on of control from the company to the crown, a process that brought with it many changes in matters of governance, finance and politics. To begin with, it cost the crown some £36 million (or about £4 billion in today's terms, at 3 per cent annual compounded rate) to take over. It then invested in maintaining close relations with the many princely states (which retained control over about two-fifths of the sub-continent) – not just in terms of trade but in military and social matters as well. This turned out to be a canny move on the part of the British, as decades later, the British army received significant contributions from the princely states, in the form of both men and money, during the two world wars.

Another result of the 1857 war was the fortification of cities that were important to the British. Having quelled the uprising, the British were alive to the fact that they were lucky this didn't set off the tsunami that could have washed away the jewel in their crown. So they set about fortifying urban centres and planning major cities on lines more familiar to them – a signature town hall, a cantonment for housing the military, an imposing railway station symbolizing British engineering prowess, majestic trees (some native and some brought from England to remind them of home), quaint bungalows for administrators that would go on to become the very symbols of the Raj, and, most importantly, neatly laid out roads.

It cannot be denied that these exercises were undertaken primarily with British interests in mind – after all, they must have seen it as investment for centuries. They took pride in stamping their excellence on their work worldwide, aiming for historic glory, perhaps best reflected in the words of the fictional Col. Nicholson (from *The Bridge over the River Kwai* by Pierre Boulle), who, when ordered to build a bridge while in captivity in Burma, intended to build one to last 600 years, while cold logic screamed that it was in his best interests to do a shoddy job: 'I know the men. It's essential that they take pride in their job ... I hope that the people who use this bridge in years to come will remember how it was built and who built it. Not a gang of slaves, but soldiers – British soldiers, even in captivity ...'

Apart from infrastructure, how can we not mention that vast, nebulous entity that the British bequeathed to us – 'The System', created for every institution to function by (and which we use today as a peg to hang all our inadequacies on) – education, railways, roadways, canals, irrigation projects, ports, the Anglo-Saxon legal system, governance, and not to forget the English language from which we derive rich dividends today? Arguable as the observation may be, according to NRI entrepreneur Kartar Lalwani, 'The girders for every bridge, the track for every mile of railway and the vast array of machinery required for India's infrastructure were all carried there [where required in India] by the same ships that helped exploit a land thousands of miles away. The engineers who laid the cornerstones for India's development from Third World nation to burgeoning industrial superpower were British.'[3]

That said, British exploitation of colonized land cannot be denied. However, instead of taking it on the chin and marching on, we take the easy route of hoisting all the blame for our condition on to our erstwhile rulers, justifiable as it may seem. Indian accounts of history clearly hold the British responsible for how they left Indians poorer and famine-prone; how they destabilized indigenous cropping patterns in favour of commercial crops to feed factories in London; how they taxed the poorest of the poor and drained out Indian revenues to pay for their own sterling debt and even to pay for an army which served only British needs, not to mention a decadent bureaucracy; and how every single piece of infrastructure that they built in India was solely aimed at serving their self-interest rather than the development of this land. Not to mention their high-handed shenanigans; history is replete with accounts of company administrators and their military alike meddling with impunity in the affairs of the princes of the Indian states.

All said, it is always problematic to view the events of a century or two ago with the lens of the present. Doing so is bound to distort our view of the motives of the then rulers in everything they did. This distortion of vision can be corrected only if we realize that irrespective of our opinion of the British civil servants – of the Raj or the East India Company – a number of British officials loved India and Indians, and did remarkable work in and for this land.

Of course, we already talked about the more obvious and visible examples in the form of town planning, infrastructure, railways, roads and so on. But what is really interesting is the little things that a few remarkable gentlemen did all by themselves – some in their spare time, some as part of active duty and some post retirement, often at odds with their own superiors. These men were not large in number, but they made a lasting difference.

And that's what this book is about – stories of a dozen British gentlemen. Wait. Why gentlemen only? As if history is not male-centric as it is, why did we choose to skew it further? You are right; it isn't fair. But neither was the time in which this book is set – for 'duty', whose call our featured few chose to go beyond, was performed by men only.

However, the role of the women of the Raj was undoubtedly impactful, and deserved discussion, during the course of which we discovered a fascinating side to the stories we were researching.

We talk about industrialization, scientific advances and systemic administration as by-products of British rule in India, but women's emancipation is perhaps the most unheralded of the developments. The role of officers' wives was, in a nutshell, to recreate a mini British society in India, and in doing so, they paved the way for Indian women to step out of their homes. And, what is more, for a cause. Our freedom struggle was as much a struggle for social independence – more so for women – as it was for political independence.

Apart from this collective influence, there were many individuals who stepped out of their defined roles – Annette Ackroyd, for instance, who started a school for girls in 1873; Flora Annie Steel, an outspoken writer and educational reformist, who also took a keen interest in the development of Indian art; and Violet Nicolson, proficient in Hindi and Urdu, with a penchant for disguising herself as a Pathan boy to explore the North West Frontier Provinces. But they were all required to do so as part of the role they played in empire building – open a school, sure, but not too enthusiastically; oppose child marriage, yes, but not too vociferously; initiate reforms in education, certainly, but not too boldly.

What we realized was that women played a complex and subtle role, creating an impact in areas far more unexpected than those that the men they were tagged to – as wives, daughters, mothers and sisters – were associated with. They were much more than these tags indicate, and their work all the more admirable because the men at least had jobs and a conviction that they were doing something worthwhile, while the women – especially the unconventional ones – had to struggle to find meaning outside domesticity.

To do their stories justice, a deeper research is called for, because there is enough material for a whole dedicated book, and that is why the scope of this work is restricted to the men who went beyond the call of duty.

And so this is a book about a dozen gentlemen, in a league of their own, who may not have had history books or even whole chapters devoted to them but whose work benefits and inspires us even today. They exemplified a work ethic that is rare, but never more relevant than today. Here were young men who ventured thousands of miles away from home under extraordinarily difficult conditions when communication and transport were both matters of months, and not seconds or hours as they are today. And they displayed a commitment that belies this fact.

For instance, who would imagine that an East India Company official well-versed in Persian, Arabic, Hebrew, Spanish, Portuguese, Germany and Chinese would turn Indologist mid-life, go on to master Sanskrit, top it by translating Kalidasa's *Sankuntalam*, *Ritusamhara* and *Manusamhita* into English, and then set up the Asiatic Society? Or that a military officer, confronted with the sight of a woman about to commit sati, would do everything in his power to stop it, while being considerate towards her and her family? The same man would go on to take the lead in establishing a system for civilian police, much of which is still in use today.

And have you heard of the visionary who almost a century before the British left India predicted exactly that and strongly advocated establishing educational institutions that preserved local culture and languages in order to equip us to eventually govern ourselves? As sitting governor, he would fight his own superiors against the sacking of a Sanskrit professor and would eventually refuse the post of Viceroy, much to our disadvantage, perhaps.

Then there was this super-human – 'prolific' seems so inadequate to describe his genius – proficient as he was in the arts, sciences, engineering and linguistics and left behind work which would have taken several lifetimes for ordinary mortals to come up with. When he beheld ancient Buddhist stupas, he knew that India had a history that stretched back a lot farther than was known at that time, and even that was indistinguishable from folklore. He took it upon himself to unravel India's past, spending much of his personal time and money on decoding ancient languages so that he could read Buddhist scripts that held the key to much of Indian history. His collection of antique coins and stunning lithographs can be seen in museums today. Apart from producing exquisite sketches of life in nineteenth century India, he designed architecturally sound bridges and repaired ancient monuments ... Who was he? Oh, just another official in the Calcutta Mint!

Back in the mid-1850s, there was this brilliant engineer who had dreamed of linking all the major rivers in India, only to be thwarted by a short-sighted bureaucracy. They couldn't, however, stop him from transforming the Godavari basin into the rice bowl of India, a remarkable feat of engineering that drew inspiration from one of the earliest irrigation systems in the world – the Grand Anicut that the Cholas had built on the Kaveri in the second century BC.

From the scorching delta we jump to the misty hills of Darjeeling, and no doubt you are thinking of tea. But there was a time when no whiff of the brew emanated from these hills, for not a single tea plant grew here! It was only after an unassuming surgeon successfully planted the Chinese variety in his backyard that Darjeeling became synonymous with tea.

Faced with ridicule and open resistance to their idea, two engineers independently dreamed of laying a railway track to connect India from coast to coast. Unfazed by failure after failure, they both worked with contrasting styles. Their work gives us fascinating insights into nineteenth century obstacles that lay in the way of a massive infrastructure project and are uncannily similar to the ones faced today.

Then there is the story of three accomplished brothers with a deep love for India. One went on to be known as the father of the Archaeological Survey of India. Another has a road in Bangalore named after him for staunchly supporting the Mysore Wodeyars, unmindful of his growing unpopularity with the British commissioner. And the third fearlessly risked his career in order to do the honourable thing by telling the true story behind the defeat of the valiant Sikhs against the British army, eventually paying the price for being forthright about unfair war practices.

His father was a general, and by all accounts, he should have had a cushy career in the army. But he chose to follow his heart, which told him to spend a lifetime painstakingly cutting up mosquitoes under a microscope. This reluctant medical student, who scraped through his exams because he would rather pen verse and compose music than study, found himself staying up nights trying to crack the mystery of the disease that had already killed millions upon millions.

Brushing away such inconveniences as lack of official approval, he spent his own time and money on this dangerous mission that required him to be the lab rat as well as the researcher. Such was his focus and determination that the only thing that could have stopped him from getting to the bottom of it was a fatal bite from one of his dappled-wing friends, and fortunately for us, that didn't happen.

The authors feel a particular kinship with this journalist – the only person featured here who is our contemporary – because he so beautifully captures all of our chaos and clumsiness with a degree of compassion. And like the other gentlemen featured here, he could have chosen to happily settle down in his home country, but chose to live in India, with love.

It is important to tell their stories because we have chosen to embrace that part of our colonial legacy that is self-destructive: a mix of high-handedness and lack of accountability that eventually led to the end of British rule in India. Instead of an unshakeable faith in mind-numbing red tape, we would do well to learn from honest and meticulous record-keeping; instead of hanging on to British systems tweaked for nineteenth century India, we would do better to tweak these for a modern India; instead of penalizing a poor performer with transfers, we could ensure better training; instead of dividing and ruling on caste and religious lines, we should reward excellence for excellence's sake.

In reading these stories we hope that in addition to an interesting glimpse into a part of our history, you will find that the struggles and triumphs of our featured gentlemen resonate, often in contrast, with today's work ethos and times.

1

Laying the Foundation of the Asiatic Society

William Jones's Tribute to Indology

1746–1794

IF YOU ARE A literate Indian and haven't heard of the Asiatic Society, well, pardon us if we say that the blame probably lies more at your doorstep than at the society's. But if you have visited Kolkata for as much as two days as a tourist and Asiatic Society still does not ring a bell, pardon us once again if we say that you must have gone out of your way to miss that majestic yellow building with tall green windows on Number One, Park Street (the first building to your left as you entered Park Street from the Maidan side). And if we are entirely wrong and you did venture inside the portals of the impressive building, you could not but have been left enormously impressed by what you observed. You must have known instinctively that you were in the interiors of a building of historical significance.

If you stroll around the two-century-old library building, you will be impressed even if you didn't know that the library boasts of books in virtually all the major languages of the world. If you log into the society's website, you will learn that the library today contains nearly 1,49,000 volumes, rich in Indology and Asiatic lore, and in standard philological and scientific serials. You may find that the printed books go back to the fifteenth century. If you happen to be an oriental scholar, you will realize that many of the volumes in the library are unique and available nowhere else in the world.

These include some of the books that were published in India in the eighteenth and nineteenth centuries. The 47,000-odd rare manuscripts are in twenty-six different scripts and languages. The library subscribes to some 80,000 journals. While the society turned in much of its precious collections to the Kolkata-based Indian Museum in 1866, it nevertheless retains an impressive collection of exquisite paintings from the Raj era, as well as sculptures, bronzes, coins and rare inscriptions. The society continues its tradition of scholarship through research, seminars and publications.

It does not take long to realize that the society is truly old – 225 years, give or take. For such an ancient institution to still be alive and active, the foundation must have been strong indeed. Who was the remarkable mortal who spawned an institution such as this? Where did he come from? What was his background? Who were his parents? What readied him to found an institution like the Asiatic Society? What was his motivation? His inspiration? Who supported him in his ambitious endeavour?

To find answers to some of these questions, we need to trek back to eighteenth century Wales to find out about the greatest non-oriental oriental scholar of all time – Sir William Jones Jr.

ANGLESEY, JANUARY 1746

William Jones Sr, our protagonist's father, at seventy-one, was all set to leave for India – on what errand, we know not. The renowned mathematician, best known for using pi (Greek symbol 'π') to represent the ratio of the circumference of a circle to its diameter, and who had hobnobbed with the likes of Sir Edmund Halley and Sir Issac Newton, was ageing but well preserved. A member of the Royal Society, and once its vice-president, Jones had Shirburn Castle, about 70 km outside of London, for his home for many years. The place was capacious and life comfortable, if not prosperous.

Mary Nix was his second wife, whom he had married (long after the death of his first wife) in April 1731. He had been fifty-six at the time of the wedding, and she, at twenty-five, had been less than half his age. But now he was seventy-one and it is at this juncture in life that William Jones Jr would be born nine months later on 28 September 1746 on the banks of the Ganga in faraway India.

William Sr spent a mere three years in India before he retired from active life on account of failing health and moved with his family to the Beaufort Buildings in Westminster in the city, where he soon breathed his last at seventy-four.

WILLIAM JONES JR, SEPTEMBER 1749

William Jones Jr was not yet three, and though already capable of thinking in three different languages – English, Greek and Latin (an early sign of the hyperpolyglot to be) – he was probably too young to grasp the enormity of his loss. In time, the young linguistic prodigy would know thirteen languages thoroughly – including Persian, Arabic, Hebrew and Chinese – and another twenty reasonably well.

There is no reason why this accomplishment cannot be

attributed to his strong-minded mother, who, with strength of character and sound sense, instilled in him the piety and curiosity of a Christian scholar. Mary was a mother centuries ahead of her time. Every time an industrious and brilliant little William Jones Jr approached her with his many questions, she would constantly respond, 'Read and you will know!' She thus encouraged curiosity in him, even while teaching him how to satiate that curiosity.

Little William, barely aware of his father's loss, was already poring over books relating to various oriental languages. At five, his imagination was captured by the inspiring description of the descending angel in the tenth chapter of Apocalypse, the last book of the New Testament. By the time the fellow was seven, his mother decided that the boy was ready to be sent to the Harrow School. The mother was so proud of her son's abilities that he was admitted to a class way beyond his tender years. Most of the classmates were ahead of him in the curriculum covered. But little William was nothing if not diligent. Besides, he had to uphold his mother's trust in him.

He systematically went about identifying the areas his classmates had an advantage in, procured the relevant books, studied them diligently, and in time, he had not only caught up with the class but he was way ahead of it. Even at this young age, he thought nothing of studying all night. If he felt sleepy, he warded off the sleep with tea. Not surprisingly, his outstanding talents and diligence were noticed very early in school. The proud master of Harrow, Dr W.M. Thackeray (the famed novelist), found little William so bright he declared that if he was left naked and friendless on Salisbury Plain, he would yet find his way to fame and riches.[1]

His studies took him far beyond the school curriculum. He was already deep into the study of law. He was able to cull out case studies from the *Institutes of the Lawes of England*, a series of legal treatises written by Sir Edward Coke, for the benefit of his classmates. Later, one of his contemporaries at Harrow, who would be Bishop of Cloyne one day, described William Jones Jr, the school boy, to have had 'great abilities, great particularity of thinking, fondness for writing verses and plays of various kinds, and a degree of integrity and manly courage [which] distinguished him even at that period. I loved and revered him; and though one or two years older than he, was always instructed by him from my earliest age'.[2]

In his last three years at Harrow, he applied himself studiously to the learning of oriental languages, including Arabic and Hebrew. He spent his vacations and holidays learning French and Italian. He entered the University College of Oxford in 1764. At Oxford, he continued to pursue oriental languages. In keeping with the traditions of the times, he had taken along a Syrian companion from London and with his help learnt Persian and polished his Arabic. He further increased his knowledge of Hebrew and added Spanish and Portuguese to his linguistic bank.

Next, finding himself in Germany, he used the opportunity to learn German, music, dancing and playing the Welsh harp. He studied Newton's *Principia Mathematica* and attended lectures by William Hunter on anatomy. Soon he mastered Chinese thoroughly, undaunted by its complex and numerous characters. By now he had begun to make a name for himself as an orientalist and a linguist. He was human enough to boast to a friend, 'With the fortune of a peasant, I am giving myself the education of a prince.'[3]

Even as an undergraduate student, he was beginning to get tutorships. In 1765, he became tutor to the second Earl of Spencer, son of the first Earl styled Baron Spencer of Althorp in 1761 (and a grand-ancestor of the late Lady Diana, Princess of Wales). Graduating in 1768, he wished to pursue his master's but could not afford the tuition fee. He therefore continued with his tutorships for the next six years, during which period he attained his master's in arts.

Just then the King of Denmark, Christian VII, was on a state visit to England. He was carrying with him a Persian manuscript on the life and times of the Persian King, Nadir Shah. Already commanding a serious reputation as an oriental scholar, William Jr was asked by Christian VII to translate the manuscript into French, which he did with élan. This was published two years later in 1770 as *Histoire de Nader Chah* and won him some critical acclaim. Within the year followed *Traite sur la Poesie Orientale* – an essay on the merits of Persian and Arabic poetry, and a French translation of ten odes of the great Persian poet Hafiz.

William Jr resigned from his Oxford tutorship, even as he continued as a fellow of the University College until 1783. In deference to the appeal of his friends, which agreed with his own inclinations, he entered himself as a student of law at the Middle Temple – the hallowed institution for Bar professionals. He was aware that law presented the only road to the highest stations in his country. He spent the whole winter attending the public speeches of the greatest lawyers and parliamentarians of the time. He devoted his leisure hours to writing a political treatise, from which he expected some reputation. At the same time, his linguistic interests remained very much alive.

A spate of publications followed. In 1771, he published *Grammar of the Persian Language* that ran eight editions until 1828 as the most authentic work on the subject. The work fell short of his own expectations of encouraging the learning of Persian among the general populace. However, his translation of the 'Tork-e-sirazi' ghazal as the *Persian Song of Hafiz* in 1771 went some way in inspiring the English poets through oriental mysticism and esotery.

ANQUETIL DU PERRON AND WILLIAM

Not long before this time, in 1755, a young man of twenty, Anquetil Du Perron, a scholar of the School of Oriental Languages in Paris, had set sail for India with the objective of bringing back home the holy books of the Parsis to translate them, since until then no authentic understanding of the works existed in Europe. Too impatient to wait for a promised government mission, Du Perron had enlisted himself as a private with the French East India Company and embarked on the long voyage. After three years of intense adventures and innumerable dangers while travelling the length and breadth of 'Hindoostan' at a time when France and England were engaged in war, he arrived in the town of Surat in the then state of Bombay and made his first contact with Parsis.

Du Perron then spent another three intense years in close proximity with the community, facing distrust, hostility and secrecy. To his great credit, he ultimately succeeded in winning their confidence. He also managed to learn Persian from them in the process. He not only managed to get a copy of their two sacred books but also acquired a good understanding of their contents. He finally returned to Paris in 1764 and deposited the holy book of Zend-Avesta and other holy works in the Royal Library. He spent the next ten years studying the books and finally in 1771 brought out the first European translation of Zend-Avesta. (He would go on to translate the Upanishads into Latin in 1804.)

This work turned out to be highly critical of the works of Oxonian scholars like Thomas Hyde, which Du Perron regarded as rather shallow. Unfortunately, however, Du Perron did not adopt a very scholarly tenor in his writings. Large segments of his 'translations' seemed to be 'transliterations'. When Zend and Persian were transliterated into French, the contents often sounded hilarious and were ripe fodder for satire at the hands of his detractors. In short, in criticizing Hyde, he had thrown a stone at Oxford while sitting inside a glass house.

This opened up a Pandora's box in Europe. The authenticity of Du Perron's works was violently brought into question. Allegations were made that much of his work had indeed been the work of the

Parsi priests and not his own. Doubts were raised as to whether Du Perron had ever even mastered the Avestan language.

At the forefront of this war was our hero, William Jones Jr.

Back to William Jones Jr

Thomas Hyde was a highly respected figure in Oxford. An affront to Hyde was an affront to Oxford. And coming from a Frenchman, it was blasphemy. As a young Oxonian, William Jr found the insult hard to swallow. Thus, soon after Du Perron's work was published, he published his *Dissertation sur la Literature Orientale*, ripping apart Du Perron's work by attacking the flippancy of its language and contents.

He argued that a sage of the standing of Zoroaster could hardly be credited with a collection of childish and ridiculous tales full of some bizarre gods and demons, much like those invoked by the Hindu priests (remember, this was the eighteenth century and a wider understanding of religions as well as political correctness was at least a couple of centuries away). Nor could a religion noted for its simplicity, wisdom and purity be full of absurd rules and laws as presented by Du Perron in his translations. Clearly, according to William Jr, Du Perron had not done his homework and his work was but a caricature of the real thing.

The publication gained him significant goodwill at Oxford. In 1772, he published a volume of poems translated from Asiatic languages as well as a couple of essays on the poetry of the Eastern nations. In the same year, he was also elected Fellow of the Royal Society.

In 1774, he published his treatise, *Poeseos Asiaticce Commentatorium Libri Sex (A Commentary of Sex in Asian Books of Poetry)*. As anticipated by him earlier, the work, which was a commentary on the liberal attitude to sex in Asia, gained him much acclaim as an authentic oriental scholar.

But even as he gained note as an oriental scholar, he wasn't making much money. After a lifetime spent, if not in penury, not in riches either, this was a matter of concern. To expand his avenues of income, he had been acquiring other skills. He had all along been a serious student of law, apart from linguistics. He was thus invited to the Bar at Middle Temple in 1774.[i] He delved not merely into the technicalities but also into the philosophy of law and by 1776 was appointed one of the sixty commissioners of bankruptcy without his solicitation.

This turned out to be a somewhat more steadily paying position. He combined his linguistic and legal skills to publish an essay on the law of bailments – a subject closely related to his then vocation. The work was received more enthusiastically in the United States than in his own country. Justice Joseph Story, who served on the US Supreme Court from 1811 to 1845, would write in 1817 in the *North American Review* that had Jones never written anything except this one essay, 'he would have left a name unrivalled in the common law for philosophical accuracy, elegant learning, and finished analysis'. High praise indeed.

In 1778, Jones proceeded to translate the speeches of Isaeus on Athenian laws of inheritance to critical acclaim.

For some time now, he had been contemplating capitalizing on his increasing reputation as an Oxford scholar for a political career. In 1780, he was all set to stand for parliamentary election representing the University of Oxford in the House of Commons. He was a liberal at a time when the tide was conservative. In particular, his liberal opinions with regards to the American civil war and slave trade were in conflict with the largely conservative mood of the time. With virtually no chance of winning the election,

---

[i] Middle Temple Hall, built between 1562 and 1573, which survived the infamous Fire of London, continues to remain at the service of the legal profession to this day.

he withdrew his candidature a day before the election, as much to avoid an ignominious defeat as to pursue his scholarly vocation. The pendulum of his interests swung back to linguistics and literature.

He was immersed once again in Arabic language and literature. In 1783, he published his translation of the ancient seven Arabic poems which were suspended on the Temple at Mecca, called the 'Moallakdt' or 'Moallakat' or the 'Mu'allaka'. The poems were in Arabic *kasidas* in iambic feet.[ii] According to Ibn Khaldun (an Arab scholar considered among the founding fathers of modern sociology, historiography and economics), in a *kasida*, each line represents a complete idea, while the means of passing from one line to another is in accordance with the genre of the ideas expressed. In short, the grammar for *kasida* is very taut, thus presenting a translator the challenge of conveying the limited mould of the verse without being hamstrung by it.

A lesser translator would seek to escape this constraint using non-conforming English words that would defeat the very grace and delicacy of the originals. But not William Jr. Interestingly, perhaps owing to the timing of his publication which coincided with the Treaty of Paris of 1783, the political significance of his work did not escape scrutiny, especially as the treaty would officially end hostilities with, and confer independence upon, the revolting Americans who were supported by William Jones.

It was about now that William Jr was appointed judge of the Supreme Court of the Judicature of Calcutta.

This had been one of his long and silently held aspirations. The position would mean, apart from an opportunity to study Indology and related fields more closely, getting a wife and living comfortably. But his liberal views and consequent antagonism

---

[ii] Kasidas are Muslim religious songs in praise and love of Muhammad, Caliphs and Companions, with iambic feet referring to the unstressed syllables followed by stressed syllables.

towards the American war delayed his appointment somewhat. Fortunately, John Dunning, later Lord Ashburton, a barrister, an influential politician and a good friend of Jones's, intervened to speed up the appointment. And for good measure, Jones was knighted on 19 March 1783.

SIR WILLIAM JONES, MARCH 1783

As a person, his contemporaries regarded Sir William Jones Jr as 'amiable and excellent, securing the respect and winning the affection of all who were fortunate enough to enjoy his intimacy'.[4] According to one of his childhood friends, Samuel Parr, an English teacher, minister and doctor of law, 'Sir William Jones is known to have united the most benevolent temper and the purest morals.'[5]

Things were working out well for Sir Jones. His long-term engagement with Anna Maria Shipley, the eldest daughter of Dr Jonathan Shipley, Bishop of St Asaph (in North Wales), was coming to fruition. He married her the very next month and set sail for India.

The newly married knight boarded the frigate, *Crococlile*. He found he was a poor sailor. The constant rocking of the vessel gave him perpetual nausea. He ate poorly. He avoided coming on to the deck as he found the rocking of the boat unbearable. But his queasy abdomen left him little stomach for any pleasures. The forced leisure combined with his ever-active mind began to result in an outline, giving shape to his plans for his future works in India. India, to him, was an enormous land mass of Hindus and Mohammedans. As a trained jurist, it was only natural that the study of the laws of Hindus and Mohammedans be uppermost on his agenda.

His time on the voyage gave him plenty of time to ponder.

Hindustan, he knew, was probably the oldest, or at least among the oldest, civilizations known to mankind. He resolved to study and document its history at length. He had found reference to the deluge not only in Christianity but also in the holy books of the ancient Sumerians, Zoroastrians and the Yiddish. He wanted to investigate if the Hindus also had a reference to the deluge in their holy texts. He was keen to explore if that one reference could perhaps bind all the religions.

He was keen to compile the verifiable facts and illustrations of the ancient scriptures of the Hindus. He knew that not much of Asiatic geography was known to his folks back home. So he was determined to include that aspect among his areas of study, along with Hindustan's political and governance systems, its taxation methods, its knowledge of various branches of science, its natural produce, its arts and its moral and ethical value systems that Europe could learn from.

Sir Jones found enough time to reflect and jot down his reflections on the constantly rocking ship. This detailed plan would soon provide an early draft for the 'Memorandum of Articles of the Asiatic Society', which he would actually launch within four months of his arrival in India.

ASIATICK SOCIETY, 1784

He set foot in India, glad to have reached his destination. Not one to take too long a set-up time, the ever-energetic Sir Jones was in a hurry to get on with his plans for Asiatic research. He sent out letters to a select set of British residents in Calcutta, inviting them to establish a society for the furtherance of Asiatic studies. Thirty of them responded to the invitation. The meeting was held in the Grand Jury room of the Supreme Court at Fort Williams, presided over by Sir Robert Chambers, Chief Justice of the Supreme Court judicature, where Sir William Jones Jr was a judge. All thirty present readily accepted membership of the society.

Within four months of his arrival in India, on 14 January 1784, he registered the Asiatick Society (the 'k' in 'Asiatick' would not be dropped until 1825). The objective of the society was to advance the cause of Asiatick research. In fact, the draft for the memorandum of articles of the society was still fresh in his mind from his recent voyage. Much of the mystery of the subcontinent, its holy books, inscriptions, literature, values, rituals, laws, polity, ancient traditions and a million other aspects of the lives of its people still remained hidden to the Europeans. Comparative philology was yet an unborn discipline. Clearly, the time was right for our polyglot to realize his dreams. The object clause in the Memorandum of Articles of the Society stated: 'The bounds of investigations will be the geographical limits of Asia, and within these limits its enquiries will be extended to whatever is performed by man or produced by nature.'

Sir Jones was helped by the fact that between 1770 and 1772, Warren Hastings – profoundly well-versed in languages and the history of India – had been instrumental in having other young and accomplished orientalists like Charles Wilkins, Nathaniel Brassey Halhed and Jonathan Duncan join him (Sir Jones) in Calcutta. Some of them joined hands with Sir Jones in giving shape to the Asiatic Society. In fact, Warren Hastings became the first president of the society, while William Jones Jr was the vice-president. But soon Hastings, terribly preoccupied with the affairs of administration, asked William Jones to assume the presidency.

Most of the orientalists thus far had either been too distracted by the challenges of their administrative responsibilities or had been thinking only in terms of individual studies and research. Sir Jones was the first one to think in terms of spawning a grand institution. He perhaps assessed the huge dimension of the work ahead better than anybody else.

At this time, only Europeans could be elected to the society. It was only after 1828 that the likes of Dwarakanath Tagore, Sivchandra Das, Maharaja Baidyanath Roy, Maharaja Bunwari Govind Roy, Raja Kalikrishna Bahadur, Rajchunder Das, Ram Comul Sen and Prasanna Coomar Tagore would be elected as members. In 1832, Ram Comul Sen would be elected 'native secretary', and after another half a century, Rajendralal Mitra would become the society's first Indian president.

But it was still 1774, and the society had just been formed. Much of its early work was flagged off by Sir Jones himself – the society's president, in fact president until death.

A priority on his agenda was to build up a sound library. Sir Jones passionately appealed to the founding members to contribute. A generous contribution soon enriched the library. As early as March 1784, the library received with gratitude seven Persian manuscripts from Henri Richardson, a Persian scholar, among the founding members of the Asiatic Society. It was followed by a contribution from William Marsden, an English orientalist, linguist, numismatist and an expert on Indonesia, of his latest book, *History of Island of Sumatra* in November 1784. The library soon gathered a critical mass and more and more rare and famed contributions followed, and thus the society laid the foundation of the first contemporary, public and seriously academic library in India.

Sir Jones was keen to procure some land to house his dream project. Unfortunately, he was unable to find a suitable stretch. Even as the society rapidly acquired fame, it had to function without a permanent address to hold its meetings, and it was perennially short of funds.

The library especially faced major problems. It lacked space to house its increasingly precious collection. Rare books, records, manuscripts, maps, drawings and lithographs, coins, antiques and other curios of historical significance were kept for safekeeping with the secretary of the society. This presented a serious risk of loss and damage to the collection. Unfortunately, it was not in Sir Jones's lifetime that a habitat would be found for the society and its library. The society would finally have its own building in 1808, when its library would be thrown open to its members and the public at the same time.

Gifts and endowments continued to pour in. The Emperor of Russia sent a royal collection. Robert Home, a former secretary of the society and the first librarian-in-charge (1804), donated his small but exclusive collection of antiques and artworks. The palace library of Tipu Sultan – the ruler of the kingdom of Mysore and a scholar, soldier and poet – sent a collection in 1808, consisting of several old and rare works. Among the gifts was an illuminated hand-painted manuscript of the Quran and an old text of *Gulistan* by Sa'di – the thirteenth century Persian poet – and manuscripts of *Padshanamah* (meaning 'Official Chronicle'), autographed by Emperor Shahjahan. The chronicle brimmed with illustrations by the greatest Mughal artists of the time. The surveyor-general, Colonel Mackenzie, gifted his own collection of manuscripts and drawings in 1822.

Thus the society had already laid the foundation of the first academic as well as public library in India. Sir Jones was satisfied that the works that had been received till then formed the nucleus of a truly great library of Indology.

A good library was only a necessary condition for scholarly research, not a sufficient one. Also required was a critical mass of scholars with enquiring minds. Thanks to Warren Hastings, he had them. His own passion for research burnt bright still. He gave eleven presidential anniversary discourses to the society – eleven being the number of years between his establishing the society and his death. Clearly, William Jones Jr took his role in the society most seriously.

Sir Jones, the Indologist, 1783-94

He was alive to the fact that if the English were to retain their power over three hundred million Hindus and Muslims, it must rest on good administration and that this could be done only if they achieved a thorough understanding of the local legal codes, which were based on the habits, religious beliefs, practices and prejudices of the people for whom they were enacted. Little time was to be lost in this pursuit.

His passion to understand the Hindu laws invariably led him to Manu – the Hindu lawgiver. He delved deep into the sage's work. He may not have lived long enough to complete his compendium of Manu's works. But he lived long enough to complete and publish his work *Institutes of the Hindu Law, or, the Ordinances of Manu, According to the Gloss of Cullùca, Comprising Duties, Religious and Civil* in 1794.

He studied the laws of succession and observed in the preface to his work, 'we may humbly presume that all future provisions for the administration of justice and government in India will be conformable, as far as the natives are affected by them, to the manners and opinions of the natives themselves; an object, which cannot possibly be attained, until those manners and opinions can be fully and accurately known'.[6]

At the same time, the philologist-cum-jurist embarked upon the twin programmes of learning Sanskrit and translating and preparing a compendium of Hindu and Muslim laws. He was the first-ever English scholar to learn Sanskrit. Such was his command over Sanskrit that by 1789, he had completed the translation of Kalidasa's *Sankuntala or* the *Sankuntalam* (but published only in 1799). He edited the text of the great Kalidasa poem *Ritusamhara*.

He translated the collection of fables *Hitopadesa* by Pilpay. He also translated *Gitagovinda*, a Sanskrit poem by twelfth century poet Jayadeva. He translated *Manusamhita* – the ancient compilation of laws by Manu between 200 BCE and 200 CE, believed to be the basis of the Hindu Law – in 1794.

Little wonder that notwithstanding his knowledge of over two dozen languages, posterity knows him best as a *Sanskrit* scholar. In 1786, he would go on to say, 'The Sanskrit language, whatever be its antiquity, is of a wonderful structure, more perfect than the Greek, more copious than the Latin and more exquisitely refined than either...'[7]

His command on languages – European and oriental alike – led him to the proposition in 1786 that there was a common source for languages ranging from Celtic to Sanskrit. This paved the way for the understanding of the Indo-European language family.

Thanks to the interest of his political masters, he turned his keen intellect to the laws of succession among Hindus and Muslims. He had been studying the subject since 1788. Four years later, he published the 'Mohammedan Law of Succession to Property of Intestates' and his 'Mohammedan Law of Inheritance'. Unfortunately, his scholarly understanding of the subject would help English usurp the realms of many a Nawab and Hindu prince, even if this was not his intent. In his words from the preface, an important consideration that had induced him to publish the work was, 'that system of duties, religious and civil, and of law in all its branches, which the Hindus firmly believe to have been promulgated in the beginning of time by MENU [Manu], son or grandson of BRAHM'.[8]

He was fascinated with Manu's erudition and comprehensive deliverance of law, but he was not oblivious to the shortcomings of his works either, as evident from his observations in the same preface, '... so clouded are the old history and chronology of India with fables and allegories, [we cannot] ascertain the precise age, when the work, now presented to the Publick, was actually composed; but we are in possession of some evidence, partly extrinsic and partly internal, that it is really one of the oldest compositions existing'.

William signs off his preface stating, 'Whatever opinion in short may be formed of MENU and his laws, in a country happily enlightened by sound philosophy and the only true revelation, it must be remembered, that those laws are actually revered, as the word of the Most High, by nations of great importance to the political and commercial interests of Europe, and particularly by many millions of Hindu subjects, whose well directed industry would add largely to the wealth of Britain, and who ask no more in return than protection for their persons and places of abode, justice in their temporal concerns, indulgence to the prejudices of their own religion, and the benefit of those laws, which they have been taught to believe sacred, and which alone they can possibly comprehend.'

Condescending though it sounds to our contemporary ears, that is perhaps as close as an English man would ever come to revere or respect India. Sir William's oriental soul seemed to come alive in India.

1794: THE LAST DAYS

Sir William was only forty-eight but his achievements were already worthy of several lifetimes. With a deep knowledge of nearly twenty-eight languages, his accomplishments as a linguist bordered on the miraculous. In life, he had allowed no difficulties to bar his course. No subject had ever been too abstruse or too trivial to warrant his deep interest. In his scholarly pursuits, he had spared no opportunity to improve his knowledge and efforts. In his relations with his God and neighbours, he had always maintained his faith. Brilliance might have been his congenital gift, but he had worked on that gift with relentless industry to give it the shape of near impossible achievement.

He had considered it his life's mission to convey at least some of his enthusiasm for and knowledge of oriental literature to the European world by means of translations of various Asiatic classics. It was essentially in this context that he had tried to solve one of the major challenges on the orthography of Asiatic words in Roman letters – for example, the writing of Hindi using the English alphabet.

His reputation even during his lifetime had been immense. The versatility of his scholarship had made him a prodigy of learning. His personal character had been spotless. He was revered for his amiability. Orientals loved him for his sympathy towards and understanding of them. They never noticed in him the contempt that his contemporaries displayed towards the 'natives'. His interaction with scholarly Indians was at once intensive and extensive.

His health was failing. His wife's health had been on the decline too and that had depressed him even more. It may be that the humidity of the tropical Calcutta ripe with mosquitoes and filth and the years of long, intense and unrelenting hours at work had all colluded in cutting his life short. He had just endured a mild Calcutta winter. It was the onset of summer. On 27 April 1794, he breathed his last – an orientalist to his dying day.

His demise was universally regretted. The directors of the East India Company paid their homage to his contributions by raising a monument to him at St Paul's Cathedral. Lady Jones, his wife, placed a monument to his memory, executed by the renowned neo-classical sculptor John Flaxman, in the ante-chapel of University College, Oxford – a fitting tribute to a great Oxonian scholar.

2

Fighting the Thugee System

W.H. Sleeman: Who Chased Thugs in His Spare Time

1788-1856

WILLIAM HENRY SLEEMAN IS an intriguing character. The more one reads about him, the more one wonders exactly what sort of man he was. Chroniclers of his deeds tend to write in extremes. On the one hand, his early biographies glorify his acts, inflating him to a larger-than-life figure; and on the other, recent historians reject all claims to greatness, seeing a colonial conspiracy to establish European superiority in such interpretations.

Best known as a civil servant who rid the land of dacoit gangs known as 'thugs', he also undertook many other initiatives, many of them with far-reaching benefits, and nearly all of them forgotten. He did, however, pursue some dubious hobbies including phrenology (the study of the shape of the human skull in the belief that it holds secrets to the individual's predisposition to crime), which is debunked today but was all the rage back then.

But we mentioned that he was an intriguing character. And so, contradictory as it may seem, he is said to have gone out of his way to acquaint himself with the customs and way of life of the people in his area, and to a large degree empathized with their troubles and beliefs – an outreach effort that was well reciprocated.

We know this not from his biographers or historians but from his own memoir, collated from notes and diaries he maintained on his travels across central India. Titled *Rambles and Recollections of a British Officer* (London: J. Hatchard and Son, 1844), this not only sheds light on the man but also provides insights into early nineteenth century life in British India.

DREAMING OF JOINING THE ARMY

Sleeman was born in 1788 to Philip Sleeman and Mary Spry Sleeman of Stratton, Cornwall. He was the fifth of nine children – eight boys and a girl. Philip was employed as a supervisor of excise, responsible for the prevention of smuggling. It may seem like a funny thing when you consider that the Sleemans were descended from the notorious Slymans (or Slemans or Slomans or Slemmans – they kept changing the spelling as they fancied) who were professional pirates in Cornwall, known to aid the smuggling of silks, laces and liquor. However, according to biographer (and British Indian army officer) Francis Tuker, 'It was not pure coincidence that persuaded H.M. [His Majesty's] Excise to offer the retired Captain Philip a chance to prove himself as adept at prevention as his fathers had been at promotion.'[1]

William grew up in the windswept coastal region off the Bristol Channel to the southwest of England, in a hamlet of grey granite houses and lime-washed cottages, riding ponies out on the moor, spending the summer months at the harbour, looking out to sea with his brothers, all dreaming of becoming sailors in the navy one day. All except one – young William had his sights set somewhere else.

Opposite the harbour stood the magnificent Pendennis Castle, a sixteenth century fort built by King Henry VIII. Every morning, the sound of drums and gunfire would reverberate around the harbour as uniformed artillerymen went through the motions of their exercise drill – firing, advancing, retreating and performing impressive routines with change of guards. This spectacle left William transfixed, but not so much his little sister, who, watching him with her hands over her ears, knew that this particular brother would go on to become a soldier, not a sailor.

And sure enough, while three of the Sleeman boys headed to sea, William prepared for the army. But soon he had to brace himself for tragedy. His brother Lewis, to whom he had said goodbye just a few days earlier, had been aboard the *HMS Weasel*, which had run into rough weather in the Bristol Channel, taking everyone down with her as she sank into the sea. As young William comforted his younger brother John, he never imagined that he would be faced with the same tragedy years later, when John too, as captain, would go down with his ship. Three years after Lewis, their father Philip died. William was just fourteen.

William's mother Mary knew that his heart was set on joining the King's Army. Her youngest son George also seemed to prefer the army over the navy. She encouraged them to study with that aim, while she tried to run the household on a diminished income. William put all his heart into his studies, concentrating on military history and political economy. It was not easy to get into the King's Army without money and influential connections, and these the family did not have.

He soon found out that a viable option for him was the Bengal Army in India, where he was told that he could get promotions without influence and the salary would be more than enough for him in India. He made his decision, but did not immediately inform his mother, for this meant that he would be stationed in India till the end of his career – may be fifty years – with only occasional visits home – enough to worry any mother. However, the most compelling reason for William's decision to join the Bengal Army was that it would enable him to save enough to send his youngest brother George to the King's Army.

In the winter of 1808, William, aged twenty, was accepted as a cadet in the Bengal Army. He immediately set about learning Hindi and Urdu and plunged deep into military history. In 1814, he served in the Nepal War, during which he saw many of his fellow soldiers succumb to injury and disease. He was also severely ill with fever, and his recovery seemed nothing short of a miracle. Consequently, he was given civil charge of the Sagar and Narmada territories in Madhya Pradesh, and thereafter he did not revert to military duties.

AN EARLY ATTEMPT TO STOP SATI

In 1828, Sleeman was given civil charge of the district of Jabalpur, Madhya Pradesh. In a short time he became popular with the locals, travelling to the remotest little hamlets, learning the language and the culture, conversing with anyone he happened to meet. His days seem to have passed in idyllic conditions, like scenes from a happy movie, as described here in his memoir:

> 'Our tents were pitched upon a green sward on one bank of a small stream running into the Nerbudda[i] close by, while the multitude occupied the other bank. At night all the tents and booths are illuminated, and the scene is hardly less animated by night than by day; but what strikes a European most is the entire

---

[i] Narmada

absence of all tumult and disorder at such places. He not only sees no disturbance, but feels assured that there will be none; and leaves his wife and children in the midst of a crowd of a hundred thousand persons all strangers to them, and all speaking a language and following a religion different from theirs, while he goes off the whole day, hunting and shooting in the distant jungles, without the slightest feeling of apprehension for their safety or comfort.'[2]

The serenity was one day broken by a rather disturbing incident. When Sleeman took charge of Jabalpur, one of his first official proclamations had been regarding the prohibition of sati. Although he had not yet received formal sanction from the government, he had issued orders to the effect that anyone found encouraging the practice, or even assisting a widow by the simple act of bringing her wood, would be punished. The following year, he heard about a sixty-three-year-old woman who had just lost her husband, Ummed Singh Upadhya, and was determined to become a sati.

The family in question was a very respectable one, and not wishing to violate a direct order had sought permission for the act. Sleeman wanted to prevent this, but there was a catch, since he did not have official sanction. This meant that he could threaten all he liked, but taking action would be risky. The most he could do was place a policeman on duty at the funeral pyre to ensure that his order was not violated.

After the last rites of Upadhya had been completed, a section of the family came to see Sleeman. They told him that the old lady would not heed anyone's words, and much as they tried to dissuade her from burning herself, she was steadfast in her resolution and would not leave the cremation ground. Some of her grandchildren were still trying hard to take her back home, they said. She had refused to leave the place, sitting by the edge of the water, refusing to eat, deaf to the pleas of her children and grandchildren. Worried that she would starve herself to death, and not wishing to prolong her miseries (and also worried that he would be charged with wanton abuse of authority), Sleeman rode out to talk to the widow himself.

He found her sitting on the edge of the water, patiently waiting for permission to mix her ashes with those of her husband. It had been four days since his demise. Sleeman approached her and tentatively suggested that she abandon the idea of committing sati. In a calm and collected voice, she told him that her soul had already left her and that nothing but her earthly frame was left. She would not eat or drink, believing that God would provide sustenance until she was given permission to carry out her wishes.

Sleeman did not relent. He tried dissuading her by pointing out that her family would be considered murderers if she took the extreme step. He said that he could see they loved her and would take care of her if she returned. To this she replied that not only would they take care of her but honour her. However, her duties towards them had ended and there was only one purpose to her life, and that was to end it.

For five days, Sleeman and the Upadhya family tried their best to convince her to go back home. Finally, the lady addressed Sleeman directly, talking clearly and with deliberation, 'I go to attend my husband, Ummed Singh Upadhya, with whose ashes on the funeral pile mine have been already three times mixed.'[3]

These were the words that finally convinced Sleeman that there was nothing further he could do; no threats or pleas would shake her conviction. Sleeman's explanation gives us a peek into the culture of the day:

'This was the first time in her long life that she had ever pronounced the name of her husband, for in India no woman, high or low, ever pronounces the name of her husband – she would consider it disrespectful towards him to do so; and it is often amusing to see their embarrassment when asked the question by any European gentleman. They look right and left for someone to relieve them from the dilemma of appearing disrespectful either to the querist or to their absent husbands – they perceive that he is unacquainted with their duties on this point, and are afraid he will attribute their silence to disrespect. They know that few European gentlemen are acquainted with them; and when women go into our courts of justice, or other places where they are liable to be asked the names of their husbands, they commonly take one of their children or some other relation with them to pronounce the words in their stead. When the old lady named her husband, as she did with strong emphasis, and in a very deliberate manner, every one present was satisfied that she had resolved to die. Looking to the sun – 'I see them together', said she, with a tone and countenance that affected me a good deal, 'under the bridal canopy!' – alluding to the ceremonies of marriage; and I am satisfied that she at that moment really believed that she saw her own spirit and that of her husband under the bridal canopy in paradise.'[4]

For Sleeman now, the choice was between watching her starve to death and allowing her to immolate herself. He saw that her family members had done their best to dissuade her from committing sati, and knew that they would honour her as the eldest lady of the household had she chosen to go back home. In his words: 'There is no people in the world among whom parents are more loved, honoured, and obeyed than among the Hindoos; and the grandmother is always more honoured than the mother. No queen upon her throne could ever have been approached with more reverence by her subjects than was this old lady by all the members of her family as she sat upon a naked rock in the bed of the river, with only a red rag upon her head and a single-white sheet over her shoulders.'[5]

Reluctantly, and against all that he held to be fair, Sleeman agreed not to prevent the lady from committing sati. He, however, set the condition that no other member of the family should in future contemplate doing the same. They agreed, and papers were drawn to the effect. The old lady was visibly uplifted by these events and began the rituals for her own cremation. She bathed, asked for a paan, and watched as the pyre was lit.

Sleeman had placed sentries in a 150-yard circle to ensure that no one else entered the area. Supported by her son and nephew, she approached the fire 'with a calm and cheerful countenance, stopped once, and, casting her eyes upward, said, "Why have they kept me five days from thee, my husband?" On coming to the sentries her supporters stopped; she walked once round the pit, paused a moment, and, while muttering a prayer, threw some flowers into the fire. She then walked up deliberately and steadily to the brink, stepped into the centre of the flame, sat down, and leaning back in the midst as if reposing upon a couch, was consumed without uttering a shriek or betraying one sign of agony.'[6]

'THUGGEE' SLEEMAN

The episode narrated above is touching because of the effort that Sleeman put in to understand the lady in question, her relatives, and the prevalent social norms (as alien to Sleeman as to many of us today), and then sensitively handling it, when he could have simply enforced the order without leaving his office.

However, what he is most famous for (or infamous, if you prefer) is his role in the suppression of what became known as 'India's murderous cult'. A slew of adventure novels sprang up when Sleeman's police activities caught public imagination at a time when the 'detective' genre of novel had not yet appeared. Philip Meadows Taylor's *Confessions of a Thug* (1839), the earliest work said to be based on a real dacoit or 'thug', led to a profusion of thuggee fiction – including Mark Twain's *Following the Equator* (1897), Jules Verne's *Around the World in 80 Days* (1873), the Indiana Jones movie *Temple of Doom* (in which the late Amrish Puri plays an atrociously written Thuggee character) and the Ismail Merchant production *The Deceivers* (in which a very young Pierce Brosnan plays a character loosely based on Sleeman). While most of the popular literature claimed to have taken inspiration from real-life dacoits of India, their exaggerated portrayal had the effect of casting doubts on the very existence of these highway robbers.

Filtering the history from the colourful narratives, we gather that central India was shaken in the 1800s by a spate of brutal highway robberies. Highway travellers were particularly vulnerable those days as they had to cover large distances on foot or horseback (the railways enter India in a later chapter).

Crouching out of sight were dacoits waiting to waylay these travellers. Once they had decided that a traveller was wealthy enough to be worth the trouble, they would slink out of their hiding places and casually join him, travel alongside for a few hours, making friends, and gaining his trust. Waiting for the right moment, perhaps after some weariness had set in, one of the dacoits would creep up from behind, slip a handkerchief around the unsuspecting traveller's neck and strangle him to death. Quickly, they would relieve him of all his possessions, leave his body lying there, and clear out of the area.

These, more or less, appear to be the facts. Popular imagination gave these highway robbers the status of a cult of religious followers of Goddess Kali. This gave rise to stories of bloodthirsty 'thuggees' holding gruesome sacrificial rituals to their goddess, as if their dacoity was divinely ordained. Popular fiction lapped all this up.

Latter-day historians have called this gross sensationalism, some going as far as to accuse Sleeman and the British officers of simply making the whole thing up. A more moderate view is that several

isolated murders may have been clubbed under the activities of
one gang. We will leave you to decide what you want to believe,
but some of the history in Jabalpur is hard to ignore.

Such as this plaque:

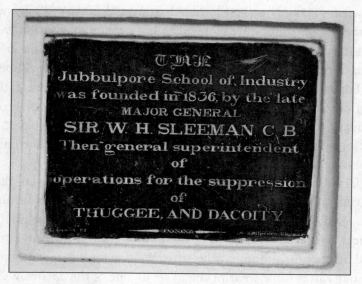

Figure 1: Plaque outside the School of Industry at Jabalpur,
founded by Sir W.H. Sleeman.

This is installed at a reformatory school in Jabalpur, where
surrendered dacoits were given education and training in various
disciplines such as making blankets, carpets, bricks and baskets.
The idea was to provide an alternative means of livelihood to the
ex-thugs and their families. As a result, some of the finest carpets
in India were handwoven in Jabalpur, as they continue to be to this
day. A specially made carpet for Queen Victoria by reformed thugs
still adorns the Waterloo Room of the Windsor Castle. Incidentally,
Sleeman had started this using his own money, in anticipation of
government funds, which came at a later date.

So it does appear that a large number of criminals were apprehended and reformed, but the numbers are perhaps a tad exaggerated, both in terms of apprehended criminals as well as their purported victims, especially by Sleeman's biographers. One of the first, J.L. Sleeman (his grandson), titled his biography *Thug, Or a Million Murders,* suggesting that this was a popular rather than a scholarly work.

Another biography by Francis Tuker is titled *The Yellow Scarf,* giving the impression that the book is more about the murderers than Sleeman. This is not the case, but the yellow scarf, purportedly the weapon of choice of the thugs, acquired a cult status of its own, starring in numerous works of action and adventure. Murder mystery as a genre of fiction had not caught on yet, and writers of the day could not resist weaving their stories around 'Thuggee Sleeman', as some had nicknamed him.

These portrayals have come in for much criticism. The sheer number of arrests he is said to have singlehandedly made seem practically impossible, as also the purported number of victims (the numbers range from a few thousands to a million). Some go so far as to say that the 'thuggee menace' was largely a product of Sleeman's imagination and encouraged by the British government in order to stamp its superiority over the 'barbaric' natives. Sleeman's portrayal as the omniscient and omnipotent 'hero' who dons the role of detective, prosecutor, judge, and reformer – a one-man show – beggars belief. Postcolonial historians have also opined that efforts of his junior officers (drawing up maps and carrying out investigations) might have been attributed to him.[7]

However, what is interesting here is not the number of arrests Sleeman made but the *manner* of these arrests. At a time when the villages around Jabalpur did not have a proper police station, let alone a police force, he conducted his investigations in a manner that laid the foundations for a professional police system in India.[8]

INDIA'S FIRST POLICEMAN

Sleeman was a keen linguist. Having learnt Hindi and Urdu on being accepted into the Bengal Army, he had, in just a few months of arriving in Jabalpur, picked up nuances of the local dialect and was able to converse fluently with the villagers. From them, he began hearing of gruesome highway robberies accompanied by murder. They were reluctant at first to confide in a 'sahib', perhaps fearing a backlash from the dacoits, but they wanted the menace to end, and seemed to have developed some confidence in their young administrator. They spoke of men armed with swords and knives (and of course the yellow scarf) not hesitating to kill for even a few valuables, dumping the bodies unceremoniously, leaving no witnesses.

Soon, even soldiers began to fall prey to highway robberies. At first, the disappearance of these soldiers was attributed to desertion. However, a dacoit in Sleeman's custody, Kalyan Singh, provided information that confirmed that soldiers had indeed been waylaid, robbed and murdered. He even led Sleeman to the spot where the bodies had been dumped. The first thirty thugs were arrested based on this information and twenty-seven bodies recovered. This was the first in a series of investigations based on the testimony of 'informers'.

Sleeman mentions another captured thug who turned informer, Syed Amir Ali (bringing into question the 'religious cult' theory, or the guilt of the accused, depending on which story you wish to doubt), whose confessions led to the establishment of a Thuggee and Dacoity Department and increased support from the government. While this is all that Sleeman himself has mentioned, many of his biographers have taken it upon themselves to accord Amir Ali the status of 'Prince of Thugs'.[9] Also known as 'Ferenghia', Amir Ali is a pivotal character in Philip Meadows Taylor's *Confessions of a Thug* and provided inspiration to many other semi-fictional works.

Having procured additional funds and manpower, Sleeman went on to make a series of arrests. A special prison was built to hold the swelling numbers of prisoners. As a deterrent, the ones who had committed the most gruesome murders were publicly hanged. The rest were subject to more interrogation, leading to more arrests. A stone pedestal in the Court House of Jabalpur still stands where Sleeman reportedly made his prisoners sit for interrogation, with the light from three windows shining directly upon them.

It might surprise many to know that India's first Police Commission was appointed in 1865, nine years after Sleeman's death. Until then, the responsibility for enforcing law and order in a district fell upon the magistrate, a British officer. Under him were 'thanedars', the native officers entrusted with the nitty-gritty of policing within their areas. There were no police officers between these two positions – quite distant from each other both in terms of power and responsibility, not to mention the fact that the magistrate was always a British officer and the thanedars always Indians. Struck by the absence of any officers between these two posts, and also the fact that the thanedars were being paid very little for the work that was demanded of them, Sleeman writes:

'These Thānadārs, and all the public officers under them, are all so very inadequately paid that corruption among them excites no feeling of odium or indignation in the minds of those among whom they live and serve. Such feelings are rather directed against the government that places them in such situations of so much labour and responsibility with salaries so inadequate; and thereby confers upon them virtually a licence to pay themselves by preying upon those whom they are employed ostensibly to protect. They know that with such salaries they can never have the reputation of being honest, however faithfully they may discharge their duties; and it is too hard to expect that men will long submit to the necessity of being thought corrupt, without reaping some of the advantages of corruption. Let the Thānadārs have everywhere such salaries as will enable them to maintain their families in comfort, and keep up that appearance of respectability which their station in society demands; and over every three or four Thānadārs' jurisdiction let there be an officer appointed upon a higher scale of salary, to supervise and control their proceedings, and armed with powers to decide minor offences.'[10]

Sleeman was of the opinion that this was a great inconsistency in governance, discussing the problems and solutions in his chapter titled 'Indian Police: Defects, and their Cause and Remedy' in his memoir, summarizing the solution thus: 'The only remedy for all this evil is to fill up the great gulf between the magistrate and Thānadār by officers.' He also bemoaned the matter of salaries, relentlessly arguing for pay hikes and promotions for the lowest rung of policemen, emphasizing that an effective and zealous workforce (and one that is not tempted to take bribes) could be constructed only by ensuring a reasonably good salary.

Sleeman did not stop at simply proposing measures. He went on to try to fill the 'great gulf' himself, while he was in charge of the elimination of the dreaded 'thugs' in the Jabalpur district, thus laying the foundation for an efficient police force. Vijai Shukul, additional director general of police (retired), Madhya Pradesh, has written about Sleeman in the *Indian Police Journal*, emphasizing the methods and structure that Sleeman put in place: 'Analytical reports of great depth, as a result of interrogation of the thugs and dacoits, informers and approvers, highlighted the modus operandi, their origin and field of operation. This was the beginning of the modus operandi system, later adopted by the police forces to detect crimes.'[11]

By 1842, the major gangs were disbanded and the highways

were safe again. While it may never be known where facts end and fiction begins as far as the 'thuggee' stories go, a reading of Sleeman's memoir indicates that he was a fair-minded man, capable of seeing all sides of a situation and taking the course of action he deemed best after making genuine efforts to understand the conventions and customs in a place that was quite alien to him. Religious motivations may have been imagined, and money may have been the prime motivator, according to a more balanced viewpoint in a recent writing by historian Mike Dash (*Thug: The True Story of India's Murderous Religion*). The possibility that innocents may have been convicted cannot be ruled out, considering that convictions were based on the evidence of informants who might have taken this opportunity to settle old scores. Mistakes might have happened then, as they happen today, and might have been brushed under the carpet, as is done today.

A VILLAGE IN HIS NAME

Sleeman continued to stay in Jabalpur, working for the welfare of the poorest peasants of the area. He had always been an admirer of rural India, the villages, the people and the abundant natural beauty. In his memoir, we see frequent comparisons between the villages and cities in India (yes, there was an urban-rural divide even back then), and his preference is clear – the villages had captured his heart. He was particularly pained when his fellow British officers spoke disparagingly about the lack of cleanliness and public spirit among Indians.

Having spent a major part of his adult life in the villages on the banks of the Narmada, Sleeman had opportunity to observe many traditional practices and a bit of history. He wrote of a large public tank flanked by majestic pipal and banyan trees interspersed with clusters of bamboo. He found out that the tank and the gardens around it had been built by a respectable agricultural capitalist some eighty years before. However, none of his relatives were to be found anywhere near that place, but the villagers would in any case take care of the gardens and maintain the tank for the larger benefit of the general public.

Sleeman has remarked in his memoir, 'Not one in a thousand of those who drink of the water or eat of the fruit knows to whom he is indebted.' Young pipal trees had begun to sprout around the area, and these were held in reverence. He was told by the villagers that 'every drop of rainwater or dew that falls to the ground from the green leaf of a fruit-tree, planted by them for the common good, proves a refreshing draught for their souls in the next world.'[12]

The tank in particular held Sleeman's attention. Amidst arid plains stood this oasis 'built using pucca masonry, at great expense, and containing the most delicious water', providing relief to parched throats and weary eyes. He rightly recognized this effort as a noble example of public spirit, and wrote to that effect in his memoir:

> 'If by the term public spirit we mean a disposition on the part of individuals to sacrifice their own enjoyments, or their own means of enjoyment for the common good, there is perhaps no people in the world among whom it abounds so much as among the people of India. [...]
> What the people of India want is not public spirit, for no men in the world have more of it than the Hindoos, but a disposition on the part of private individuals to combine their efforts and means in effecting great objects for the public good[ii].'[13]

Sleeman did what he could to foster this spirit. In 1820, he had 96 acres of land procured from the government for landless labourers

---

[ii] An observation as valid today as then. Raghunathan in his book *Games Indians Play* (Penguin, 2006) refers to the same characteristic as us Indians being 'privately smart and publicly dumb'.

in his jurisdiction for the purpose of settling them and securing their future. Out of this settlement was born the small village of 'Sleemanabad', aptly named in his honour.

Sixty-five kilometres from Jabalpur, proceeding towards Benares on National Highway 7, you will find this hamlet nestled between Sihora and Teori. Past the railway station, as you enter the town, you will be greeted by a large memorial standing next to a small shrine. Behind the shrine, painted on a wall, is a notice detailing the history of Sleemanabad.

Figure 2: Sleemanabad's history on a wall.

The notice in Hindi, written by C.N. Dubey, sub-divisional officer of Sleemanabad, explains the work done by Sleeman in the elimination of thugs and making the place safe.

There is also a charming piece of history associated with a lamp, kept burning in a small shrine in this village.

In 1828, Sleeman married Amélie Josephine, daughter of Count Blondin de Fontenne (a French nobleman who had managed to escape the Revolution, leaving his considerable wealth behind). In 1832, while on a tour of the surrounding areas, they visited the village of Khoka that would later be named in his honour. An elder of the village welcomed them, and on hearing that they had been married four years and were yet without children, was deeply concerned. He therefore led them to an ancient shrine and told them that couples who prayed there were soon blessed with children. Sleeman jokingly told him that if his prayers were answered, he would donate a large sum of money to the shrine.

The following year, Amélie gave birth to a son, whom they named Henry Arthur. Sleeman kept his promise and made a generous offering to the temple. To show their gratitude, the priests lit a small lamp for Sleeman, to be kept burning forever in his memory. A century later, when his grandson James Sleeman visited the shrine, he found it burning. Moved by the warm welcome he was accorded by the villagers – he was escorted in a procession through triumphal arches and streets lined with buntings – he said, 'where else in the world today would one find such generous expression of gratitude for services rendered over a century ago?'[14] He went on to visit the police station designed and built by his grandfather, saw the Darikhana (school of rug-making industry), spoke to descendants of thugs, and described his visit as something straight out of the pages of *The Arabian Nights*.

Visitors to the shrine up until the 1990s have seen this lamp burning. However, at present this practice seems to have been stopped. A century and a half of homage is no small achievement, but, more importantly, speaks volumes. One may choose to doubt the stories of the thugs, but that lamp tells a different story.

SLEEMAN THE DINO MAN

Sleeman did not confine his diggings to criminal investigations alone. The central province of India where Sleeman served is part of a large volcanic rock formation – the largest one on earth, in fact – called the Deccan Traps. Volcanic eruptions that occurred over 65 million years ago created multiple layers of solidified basalt, going down to a depth of 2,000 metres into the earth. (The term *trap* is derived from the Swedish word for 'stairs', because this is how the landscape looks – like a series of step-like hills).

Sleeman's house in Jabalpur had a beautiful view of the Bara Simla Hill. He observed that the patterns of stratification of basalt over sandstone at one point corresponded exactly with the patterns some 20 or 30 miles across the valley. Upon discussion with a geologist, he learnt that this was due to the flow of lava, which in liquid state filled the hollows, but upon hardening got decomposed and washed away while the basalt was left, containing in it some interesting things.

After some digging, Sleeman was thrilled to discover petrified remains of plants and small trees, some with roots, branches and leaves intact. He even found a grove of silicified palm trees through which the officers of the nearby military station had been riding every day, not realizing that the 'stones' around them were part of a fossilized forest.

'It was some time before I could convince them that the stones which they had every day seen were really petrified palm-trees,' says a note in his memoir.[15]

But Sleeman himself did not realize the importance of his next find – a few huge bones in fossilized rock that he thought to be of some animal – which he mentions in just one sentence in his memoir. He did, however, keep the bones, which were later sent to the Indian Museum in Calcutta. Some thirty years later, they were identified to be reptilian, and still later, possibly dinosaurian. Initially attributed to a single dinosaur, it is now believed that these bones possibly belong to different dinosaurs of the Titanosauridae family. This makes Sleeman the first person to discover dinosaur fossils in the Deccan Traps.[iii]

[iii] Subsequently a number of fossils have been found in this area, not just of dinosaurs, but of early ancestors of frogs and mollusks as well, making it a rich source of study. It has been theorized that the volcanic explosion in this

In telling the story of William Henry Sleeman, we have strived to achieve a balance, keeping in mind nineteenth-century awareness and norms while throwing light on some lesser-known facts. Francis Tuker, in his preface to Sleeman's biography, puts forth his reasons: 'It has until recently been the custom for writers and speakers in England to portray their countrymen in British India as a people for whom Indians at large had an ill feeling. Of late, however, the many British newcomers to India or Pakistan have been pleasantly surprised at the warmth of the welcome they receive and at the good feeling there is for the British. They have wondered why this should be. This life of William Henry Sleeman, so typical of his kind, may help towards explaining the existence of this fund of goodwill and may afford a useful introduction to the great country of India.'[16]

The last line above particularly sums it up for us. Reading about this British officer, his work, and his observations of life in India was in parts as enlightening to us as it must have been to the originally intended European audience.

---

area was responsible for wiping out the dinosaurs, and not a meteorite, as had been supposed earlier.

3

The Founding Father of Modern Indian Education

Mountstuart Elphinstone: The Educationist Governor of Bombay

1779–1859

IT WAS A QUIET day in Benares. Winter had set in, and the city was basking in the soft January sunshine. The year was 1801.

A short distance away from Benares was a pretty little settlement markedly different from the city. Tidy streets led to immaculate bungalows with open grounds, neat gardens, breezy verandahs and extensive terraces, giving an impression of spaciousness in a city (described by Lord Thomas Babbington Macaulay) of 'half a million human beings crowded into a labyrinth of lofty alleys'.[1]

This little suburb was created to house the many British officers residing in Benares. Into this little oasis they had brought a bit of home, as John Francis Davis, a British diplomat and the second governor of Hong Kong, described: 'In style they somewhat resemble the villas and country seats of our English gentry, with such modifications as may be demanded by the climate. Insulated within their own grounds, the four sides are open to the winds, while a plentiful supply of Venetian blinds serves to exclude the excess of the sun's rays.'[2]

In one of these houses, decidedly against his wishes, lived a non-European, the deposed Nawab of Oudh[i] Wazir Ali Khan. Wazir Ali, a few years before, had staked claim to the throne following the demise of the Nawab Asaf-ud-Daula. However, as he was only an adopted son of Asaf-ud-Daula, he had just been deposed by the British and his claim for the throne rescinded. Asaf-ud-Daula's brother, Sadat Ali Khan, was installed as the new Nawab, and Wazir Ali placed under surveillance at one of the houses in the suburbs of Benares. To all external appearances, he was no prisoner – he would visit the resident officer for tea, and was even allowed his regular retinue of 200-odd followers, and a victory drum (nagada) preceded him whenever he went out, to indicate that he was a man of high rank – but he was under house arrest all the same.

In charge of keeping an eye on Wazir Ali was the British Resident[ii] to Benares, George Cherry. Suspecting that a scheme for wresting the throne back was brewing in the young ex-Nawab's mind, he decided to move him to Calcutta, where his meetings with conspirators could be kept under check. Wazir Ali was furious as he had indeed been hatching a plot for insurrection, and everything had rested on his being present in Benares. He made his displeasure known loud and clear, but was ignored. Smarting from the disgrace, this tempestuous young prince decided to retaliate.

---

[i] The colonial name for Awadh.

[ii] British Residents were appointed to princely states as political agents in charge of maintaining diplomatic ties with the native rulers (and of course ensuring their allegiance to the East India Company).

Two days before he was scheduled to leave for Calcutta, Wazir Ali Khan decided to pay a visit to the resident officer, but this was a visit like no other.

Cherry, in his sitting room, heard the sound of Wazir Ali's drums approaching. A 200 strong retinue, armed with swords and guns, carrying lighted torches, some on horseback and some on foot, accompanied the ex-Nawab. If Cherry was afraid, he did not show it. He maintained protocol and welcomed the party and offered them tea. Wazir Ali refused to touch his tea. He instead spoke of all the humiliation he had endured, and his voice rose in anger. All around him, tempers flared.

A point came when all niceties were thrown to the wind and swords drawn. All of a sudden, Wazir Ali, rising from his chair, struck at Cherry with his sword, mortally wounding him. Whether this was done in the heat of the moment or whether it was a premeditated move, we will never know, but his followers, taking it as a signal, also drew their swords and proceeded to massacre everyone in the building.

The armed men then went on the rampage in the little British suburb, setting fire to houses and shops, and killing every European in sight.

Among the few who survived was a mild-mannered assistant to the magistrate, Mountstuart Elphinstone, then just barely out of his teens. In his sixteenth year, the lad had been commissioned to the Bengal Presidency when his uncle, William Elphinstone, who commanded a ship under the East India Company, used his influence to procure for Mountstuart a position in Bengal at such a young age.

Child in a Castle

Mountstuart was the fourth son of John Elphinstone (the eleventh Lord of Elphinstone) and his wife Anne Ruthven. He was born on

6 October 1779 at Dumbartonshire, Scotland, and grew up mostly in Edinburgh Castle, the family's official residence when John Elphinstone was the governor. Growing up, he spent his time in the company of French prisoners housed in the castle's dungeons, wearing his hair long in imitation of their style, and singing their revolutionary songs.

He was surrounded by family members (present as well as past) with distinguished military and academic careers. One of his ancestors, Bishop Elphinstone, had founded the University of Aberdeen. Mountstuart's own father had fought under Major General James Wolfe, best known for his victory over the French in the battle of Quebec during the Seven Years' War in Canada (1756-1763). Plenty of uncles were in the navy, one of them going on to become a director in the East India Company, and his brothers were in the army. So it was no surprise that he had always dreamed of having a military career growing up.

Fate, however, had other things in store for him. After attending high school in Edinburgh for a short while, he was packed off to a prestigious boarding school in Kensington. He was fourteen. The very next year, he heard from his uncle, the director in the East India Company, that a clerical position at the Bengal Presidency had been procured for him.

From his boarding school in Kensington he wrote to his mother, telling her of this appointment and his decision to accept it in spite of his inclination to join the army. Perhaps the demise of his father a few months ago prompted him to take up this offer of employment at the ripe age of fifteen.

'My dear Mama – I am extremely happy to inform you that my uncle has got me appointed to Bengal, and on Saturday last he sent for me home, and told me that I was to go with this fleet, which sails in six weeks [...] I am, you may be sure, very much obliged to my uncle, and very happy to be appointed, in spite of all the cockades in this world, which are never to be compared to Bengal. But the worst of all is that I will not be able to return to Scotland for want of time, and so have no possibility of seeing you and my sisters.'

His reference to 'all the cockades in the world' is an indication of how much he had wanted to join the army. But this opportunity for employment was not to be passed up. The last line of his letter displayed a maturity beyond his years as he declared: 'If I am appointed, I shall think no more of the army.'[3]

It is fascinating to read how this man, with limited formal education and no army training whatsoever, went on to make a name for himself in precisely those two fields – as political agent and aide-de-camp during war, and as a builder of modern education in India.

THE TEENAGER LANDS IN INDIA

After a journey lasting more than eight months, he landed in Calcutta on 26 February 1796. He was appointed a writer (archaic for clerk), and flitted across a series of subordinate positions, sticking to his duties with diligence despite his young age, not falling prey to the temptations and philandering that so many single young men of the company were so easily drawn to.

It was for this reason, in fact, that Lord Charles Cornwallis, the well-known colonial administrator, had established the College of Fort William 'to give some chance of culture to the raw youths who filled the lower branches of the establishment'.[4] Elphinstone took full advantage of this institution and its library in particular. He studied Greek and Latin classics in earnest, and embarked on learning Persian and Hindi, whilst about him his colleagues indulged in the usual excesses of drinking, gambling and spending evenings in the company of the famed 'nautch girls'.[iii]

[iii] Alarmed by this debauchery, and in order to keep British officers away from

A few months later, he was sent to Benares on his first posting as assistant to the magistrate. And so his days passed uneventfully for a time, toiling at the desks during the day and reading copiously through the night, until the monotony was rudely broken when the followers of the deposed Nawab Wazir Ali Khan wreaked mayhem on the British settlement in Benares.

Escaping by the skin of his teeth, Elphinstone recorded the event in his diaries, praising the stout defence of the magistrate Samuel Davis (a Sanskrit scholar), who stood guard with a spear at the entrance to the terrace of his house, where his family[iv] had huddled to escape the wrath of the mob.

In 1801, he was posted to Poona, in the Bombay Presidency, at the other end of India. His work in the Bombay Presidency, particularly in the area of education, is regarded the foundation for the economic progress that would be propelled by the empowerment that education provided. But this would come a little later.

EARLY DAYS IN BOMBAY PRESIDENCY

To make the journey from Calcutta to Poona, Elphinstone took the rather circuitous route along the east coast, going all the way to Madras, before cutting across the Deccan plateau towards

---

the comforting arms of brown mistresses that produced inconvenient offspring of mixed blood, the East India Company in the late-nineteenth century began shipping fleets of young British women to India, with the express purpose of fixing suitable matches for officers. These girls' travel expenses were taken care of, and they were allotted living expenses for one year, by which time they were expected to find a husband.

[iv] Among the family members was a four-year-old boy, John Francis Davis, who later wrote a detailed account of this incident and the history behind it in a book titled *Vizier Ali Khan; Or The Massacre of Benares: A Chapter in British Indian History.*

Poona. He arrived at a turbulent time. Colonel Arthur Wellesley (brother of the then governor-general) was involved in a campaign against the fractured Maratha kingdom. The French were tempted to attack India's south-west at this point, and Wellesley was keen on establishing British supremacy in the region. The British government had imposed heavy taxes on the Peshwa king in order to bolster the government coffers to help fund the peace. And the king, in turn, imposed heavy taxes on his people – who ended up doubly exploited, leading to widespread unrest in the region. War became inevitable.

Posted as an assistant in the diplomatic service, Elphinstone acted as a virtual aide-de-camp (rare for a civilian) to the colonel during the Anglo-Maratha wars. In this capacity, he displayed such deep knowledge of strategy and military tactics that Wellesley was prompted to remark that Elphinstone should have been a soldier, not a civil servant. Of course, the defeat of the Marathas was not a happy outcome from the Indian point of view – but then, we will not indulge in theorizing on what *might* have happened, and instead stick to recounting what *did* happen, and leave it to you to decide if any good came of it.

In 1808, Elphinstone was sent to Afghanistan to handle the threat of a French invasion from the north-west frontier. He spent the next few years in Afghanistan, deftly executing his somewhat sketchy brief, for the situation was complicated: British relations with Persia had to be carefully balanced with his negotiations with the Afghan rulers. In the end, he did succeed in signing a short treaty that paved the way for perpetual friendship and non-interference with the Afghans.

Elphinstone returned to India in 1811 and was appointed resident with the Peshwa at Poona. Following a series of wars between the Marathas and the British, and the subsequent overthrow of the Peshwa, Elphinstone was put in charge of settling the newly acquired territories. He must have done a good job, because in a highly unusual move, a servant of the East India Company was appointed Governor of Bombay Presidency in 1819. His time as governor was to be one of the most peaceful times in British Indian history.

One of his goals as administrator was to ensure that his policies were in tune with Maratha sentiment, so that he preserved traditional learning institutions (including those part of temples and madrasas), restored lands to provincial rulers, bestowed judicial powers on village headmen for effective administration of local law, and, of course, pioneered a system of education for Indians at a time when British public opinion was not entirely convinced of the need for it.

Elphinstone's priority was to achieve lasting peace in the region, and he strongly believed that taking well-meaning developmental measures was the right path to forging good relationships. Having served in the Bengal Presidency earlier – the seat of learning at that time – Elphinstone had seen the advantages of education for Indians as well as British civil servants as this resulted in greater Indian participation in government affairs and greater understanding of governance, leading to greater goodwill for the British.

This was a scene of the changing times in India. The East India Company had staked claim as the rulers of India a century ago. Through these one hundred years, their policy had been one expressly opposed to the education of the 'natives'. However, a group of British scholars (mostly consisting of Scotsmen influenced by the Scottish Enlightenment – prominent among them, Sir Gilbert Elliot-Murray-Kynynmound [later, Lord Minto], Thomas Munro, John Malcolm, and Mountstuart Elphinstone[5]) disagreed. These administrators were scholars who took the time to study India's classical languages and understand the culture which produced such great literature. Most of them were quite proficient in Sanskrit and Persian, along with Hindi and the language of the region they worked in.

And they did much more than just learn a couple of languages – they felt the richness of India's history and did much to let the world know that. (The establishment of the Asiatic Society by Sir William Jones was a direct result of this.) These scholars harboured, in Malcolm's words, 'a compassion for fallen greatness' and their aim was to restore India's moral independence.[6] At the same time, they knew that continued British presence in India would be possible only by actively engaging Indians in governance, and recognized that education was the first step towards this.

To Educate the Natives or Not – That Was the Question

The first proposal for sending schoolmasters to India was put forth in 1792 before the Court of Directors of the East India Company, to which their response was, 'Having just lost America from our folly, in having allowed the establishment of Schools and Colleges, it would not do for us to repeat the same act of folly in regard to India; if the Natives required anything in the way of education, they must come to England for it.'[7]

A couple of decades later, a second proposal was put forth, mostly by the British officers stationed in Bengal. This time, it was given due consideration and a sum of 'not less than one lac rupees'[8] was ordered to be set apart for the purpose of imparting education to the natives of India. The first effect of this was seen in Bengal, which produced many leading thinkers of the Bengal Renaissance, prominent among them Dr Raja Ram Mohan Roy.

Elphinstone wanted to replicate this story in Bombay, but with a twist. He understood that effective execution of British policies was possible only by a large class of educated Indians in civil service. Since the schools in Bengal were engaged mainly in linguistics, he proposed imparting classical English, along with European sciences. His vision was to create a class of Indians educated in English in the sciences, the knowledge of which they could then impart to the masses, especially in the villages, in the local language.

Meanwhile, a group of scholars in Europe began to advocate a programme of 'anglicizing' the Indian populace. They rejected the orientalists' view that India's past had once been glorious, and instead held that a progressive India could be made possible only by separating the country from her past and introducing Western ideals, way of life and religion. The advent of evangelists and missionaries also began at the same time, and they supported this view.

Now Elphinstone was no Anglicist – in fact, being well versed in Indian languages, he probably leaned more towards the side of the orientalists – but the overwhelming mood of the day was in favour of Anglicization. This was a time when much of India's history was unknown – the Indus Valley was unheard of, Ashoka was the stuff of myths and legends, the Gupta Empire and much of south Indian history were yet to be discovered (in a later chapter, we will see how Sir Alexander Cunningham helped in digging up much of our past), erstwhile kingdoms were crumbling, no strong leadership emerged anywhere in the country, and it certainly seemed as if it was up to the Englishman to show us the light. Anglicizing education seemed to be the best place to start.

ELPHINSTONE'S MINUTE ON EDUCATION[9]

In 1824, Mountstuart Elphinstone presented to the Court of Directors a Minute on Education. He started with the basics. First, construct schools, he said. Then recruit sufficient teachers and print and distribute books. Make things interesting by awarding proficient scholars, providing lucrative employment to graduates, and providing other incentives to learn, he continued. These may seem like very simple points, but they speak volumes about what the situation was like: the very foundation for an education system had to be laid.

When it came to the question of 'anglicizing' education, this is what Elphinstone had to say:

'If English could be at all diffused among persons who have the least time for reflections, the progress of knowledge by means of it would be accelerated in a tenfold ratio, since every man who made himself acquainted with a science through the English would be able to communicate it in his own language to his countrymen. At present, however, there is but little desire to learn English with any such view. The first step towards creating such a desire would be to establish a school at Bombay, where English might be taught classically, and where instructions might also be given in that language on history, geography, and the popular branches of science.'

Where Elphinstone sharply disagreed with the Anglicist view was in his belief that it was important to preserve the local culture and languages. He was careful to stress that no part of the education should infringe upon the religious beliefs of any community, and while teaching ethics, advocated borrowing from the ancient texts of India.

According to James Sutherland Cotton in his book *Mountstuart Elphinstone and the Making of South-Western India*, 'One of his first plans at Bombay (1820) – which was thwarted by the opposition of his colleagues in Council – was to graft a native college on the proposed European one, so as to educate native instruments of government by the side of young civil servants, and likewise to preserve and encourage native learning.'[10]

Elphinstone was constantly in touch with Sir Thomas Munro, who was in the process of empowering farmers in the Madras Presidency by introducing a new system of revenue which would greatly benefit the labourers and which still stands the test of time. He attached special importance to the teaching of the sciences with emphasis on the medical sciences. He suggested recruiting British civil surgeons for the purpose and providing incentives in the form of prize money and employment to Indians who acquired medical knowledge.

He understood the need to preserve the native institutions of learning, and while not exactly advocating teaching in the vernacular, he was clear that classical literature of all languages ought to be taught in schools. A great lover of Greek literature, he said that it was important to preserve the ancient languages even though they may not be spoken any longer, because the ancient classics would never cease to hold pertinent lessons for generations to come.

A Man with a Vision

Elphinstone had a vision that was ahead of his time, which not too many people were yet ready to appreciate or understand. That is perhaps why he received neither the accolades (heaped by the British on the likes of Lord William Henry Cavendish-Bentinck, the governor-general of India from 1828 to -1835, a soldier-statesman) nor the admiration (heaped by Indian historians on Indophiles like William Jones) he deserved.

Be that as it may, what is striking is his candid view, expressed in 1854, that the British would eventually leave India. In a letter to Sir T.E. Colebroke (his biographer) he wrote:[11]

'The moral is that we must not dream of perpetual possession, but must apply ourselves to bring the natives into a state that will admit of their governing themselves in a manner that may be beneficial to our interest as well as their own and that of the rest of the world; and to take the glory of the achievement and the sense of having done our duty for the chief reward of our exertions.'

In another communication, he echoed this view:

'A time of separation must come; and it is for our interest to have an early separation from a civilised people, rather than a violent rupture with a barbarous nation, in which it is probable that all our settlers and even our commerce would perish, along with all the institutions we had introduced into the country.'

Perfectly aware that the Court of Directors of the East India Company did not share his view, he intended his measures to take effect very slowly, so that it would not, in his words, 'alarm' the directors. In a letter dated 1826, he wrote:[12]

'Our object [...] must be to gradually relinquish all share in the civil administration, except that degree of control which is necessary to give the whole an impulse and direction. The operation must be so gradual that it need not even alarm the Directors for their civil patronage; but it ought to be kept in mind, and all our measures ought to tend to that object. The first steps are to commence a systematic education of the natives for civil offices, to make over to them at once a larger share of the judicial business, to increase their emoluments generally, and to open a few high prizes for the most able and honest among them.'

As it was, he had a hard time fighting to preserve the Poona College, and in particular the Sanskrit department, which he stressed was not running on the company's revenue. Although he was not a scholar in Sanskrit, he was passionate about preserving classical languages for their poetry. In this regard, the Minutes on Education (1824) stand testimony to his deep understanding and respect for India and its culture. Specifically with reference to some questions on the appointment of a Sanskrit professor in Poona College, he said:

'... At no time, however, could I wish that the purely Hindu part of the course should be totally abandoned. It would surely be a preposterous way of adding to the intellectual treasures of a nation to begin by the destruction of its indigenous literature; and I cannot but think that the future attainments of the natives will be increased in extent as well as in variety by being, as it were, engrafted on their own previous knowledge, and imbued with their own original and peculiar character...

'... At first sight it seems of little practical utility, but on a closer examination it will probably appear worthy of being looked on with more favour. [One should be] aware how large a portion of the Hindu literature is formed by Sanscrit poetry. It is this part which seems to have the most intrinsic merit, and which has called forth the enthusiastic admiration of no mean judges among ourselves. It is this part also which it is both most practicable and most desirable to preserve. Even without the example and assistance of a more civilised nation, the science possessed by every people is gradually superseded by their own discoveries as they advance in knowledge, and their early works fall into disuse and into oblivion. But it is otherwise with their poetry: the standard works maintain their reputation undiminished in every age, they form the models of composition and the fountains of classical language; and the writers of the rudest ages are those who contribute the most to the delight and refinement of the most improved of their posterity.'

It was this quality of noble plea that resulted in the retention of the professorship of Sanskrit in Poona College.

This was divergent from the direction that education was

taking in Bengal, where the battle between the Orientalists and Anglicists had come to a head, particularly on the issue of medium of instruction to be used in schools. Lord Macaulay had just presented a Minute on this, advocating the Anglicist approach to use English across all Indian schools. This was passed without much debate, even if the debate has refused to die down nearly two centuries later.

As Governor of Bombay, however, Elphinstone begged to differ, and for a long time, a judicious balance of teaching in English and the vernacular was continued.

As an interesting aside, when Elphinstone was back in England, and happened to live for a brief while in Albany, on the same floor of his apartment lived Thomas Macaulay. Says Charles Macfarlane, a friend of Elphinstone (in his book *Reminiscences of a Literary Life*):

'Three East Indians were living there at the same time, and in the same corps de logis, and I believe on the very same floor – Mr Elphinstone, Lord Glenelg, and Thomas Babington Macaulay, whom people will persist in calling the Historian, although with him History is little more than a romance and a political satire. I know that the three were every day ascending and descending the same staircase. Their apartments were in the principal block of the building—that which, in front, looks on the open courtyard and on Piccadilly. With easy, indolent, good-natured Lord Glenelg the case was different; but I believe that there was not, and never could have been, much sympathy between two men so different as Macaulay and Elphinstone.'[13]

RETIREMENT – AND WHAT MIGHT HAVE BEEN

Elphinstone resigned from the post of Governor of Bombay Presidency in 1827, in order to heed to another calling. His travels all over India and the deep understanding he had gained were simply crying out to be put in book form – and the result was a two-volume *History of India*, published in 1841. However, for this book to materialize, he declined the post of Governor-General of India, not once, but twice.

Makes you wonder what course our history might have taken had this man been at the helm during a crucial shifting of power. For this was before the First War of Independence of 1857, when the East India Company represented the Government of India. Post 1857, the administration changed hands and the British Crown took over. Had Elphinstone been governor-general, would the conflagration have been avoided? Would we have seen a smoother and earlier restoration of sovereignty for the Indian subcontinent? While there can be no end to speculation of this sort, we can be sure of the goodness of his thought, best summarized by this line in a letter to his friend Edward Strachey in 1821:[14] 'It is not enough to give good laws, or even good courts; you must take the people along with you, and give them a share in your feelings, which can only be done by sharing theirs.'

A couple of decades after he retired, he heard of a proposal to set up a college in Bombay in his honour. In his characteristic manner, he is said to have remarked, '*Hoc potius mille signis*' – it is a sign.

The college grew in reputation, and it is a fitting tribute that among the notable alumni of the Elphinstone College overlooking the Arabian Sea are such stalwarts as Bal Gangadhar Tilak, Dadabhai Naoroji, B.R. Ambedkar and J.N. Tata, among others, who went on to shape a vital part of the Indian psyche as we went through tumultuous times.

We leave you to ponder on something Elphinstone said around the mid-1800s, which gives us not only a snapshot view of the socio-economic conditions of our country at that time but also makes us vaguely uncomfortable that precious little has changed:

'It is difficult to imagine an undertaking in which our duty, our interest, and our honour are more immediately concerned. It is now well understood that in all countries the happiness of the poor depends in a great measure on their education. It is by means of it alone that they can acquire those habits of prudence and self-respect from which all other good qualities spring; and if ever there was a country where such habits are required, it is this. We have all often heard of the ills of early marriage and overflowing population; of the savings of a life squandered on some one occasion of festivity; of the helplessness of the ryots which renders them a prey to money-lenders; of their indifference to good clothes and houses, which has been urged on some occasions as an argument against lowering the public demands on them; and finally, of the vanity of all laws to protect them when no individual can be found who has spirit enough to take advantage of those enacted in their favour. There is but one remedy for all this, which is education.'

As we said, who knows what course our country might have taken, had this man been at the helm ...

4

Extending Indian History

James Prinsep: The Multifaceted Genius

1779–1859

IF EMPEROR ASHOKA IS a familiar name to an average schoolkid in India today, if we have the Ashoka Pillar as our national symbol, if the history of Buddhism in India has been pushed back to its origins, we would do well to remember the untiring work of the famed numismatist and philologist, James Prinsep. His brief life, spanning no more than forty-one years, encapsulated the works of many lifetimes.

Ashoka's Pillars, comprising four segments, were sculpted from spotted red and white sandstone or hard grey sandstone, quarried somewhere near Mathura and Chunar (near present-day Varanasi), and moved great distances to the northern parts of the country, where they are found today. The pillars stand some 40 to 50 feet tall, weigh up to 50 tonnes and date back to the third century BC.

Of these, some nineteen pillars survive and are in various states of disrepair.

The edicts of Ashoka, encapsulating Buddhist teachings, are carved on them in ancient script. These inscriptions, particularly those found on the pillars at Delhi and Allahabad, were published in several volumes of the Asiatic Society's proceedings during the time of Sir William Jones, whom we know well by now. Decrypting these inscriptions had perplexed Indologists for a long time, and Ashoka's identity itself remained rather vague.

Finally, it would be left to James Prinsep to decode these inscriptions, based on his deep understanding of ancient scripts, honed by his hobby of numismatics. The edicts conveyed through these inscriptions proved to be issued by a king named Piyadasi, meaning the beloved of the gods. Thanks to the decryption of the script on these pillars by Prinsep, it was only a matter of time before more and more edicts of the same king were translated, one of which, in 1915, clearly identified King Piyadasi as none other than Ashoka.

Who was this James Prinsep? What made him the Indologist that he turned out to be? What made him interested in India and its history? Let us rewind to the time of James's father, John Prinsep.

JOHN PRINSEP: THE FATHER

John Prinsep, born in 1746, was the tenth child and seventh son of a vicar of Bicester in Oxfordshire, England. We learn from British parliamentary records (as, later in life, John Prinsep would be a parliamentarian), that by the age of sixteen, young John had 'apprenticed with William Hird, skinner, of London'.[1] He leveraged his apprenticeship to engage in fabric trade with the East India Company. Such was his acumen that before long he was advising the company on improving its fabric business. In 1771, he contemplated a change of scene and career and boarded an East India Company ship, as an officer cadet, bound for Calcutta.

He arrived at the Calcutta docks nearly penniless, but equipped with some valuable introductions. He discovered that unlike in London, in Calcutta his introductions went a long way. They opened doors; they got him friends; they earned him hospitality; and all in all made his life smoother. Among his early well-wishers was Warren Hastings, who had only just taken charge as the Governor-General of Bengal, and who helped John opt out of his commission in 1772 in order to embrace a far more rewarding career in indigo plantation and trading. By 1773, he was Alderman (or a member of the municipal council) and was learning to leverage his connections astutely.

Apart from India, North America was the other major exporter of indigo to the British, with much of the indigo coming from South Carolina. However, just about this time, news was in the offing that thirteen British colonies in North America had broken away from the empire to form the United States of America. The revolutionaries had thrown out British officials and suo moto declared independence, setting up a government in each of the thirteen colonies and leading to the American Revolutionary War. Anticipating glitches in the American export of indigo to Britain, in 1779 John Prinsep started the cultivation and manufacture of indigo for export back home. He set up a plantation in Nilgang, near Barrackpore.

The revolution all but stopped the American exports of indigo, leaving the British market wide open to Indian indigo planters like John Prinsep. The right man at the right place at the right time, if ever there was one! And so profitable was the indigo export and so powerful were John's connections that he promptly opened a government-approved mint for copper coins in 1773. That he also controlled the copper mines in Rotasgarh (in present-day Bihar) was the icing on the cake.

From here on, John Prinsep was on a roll. He used his cloth trading background to the hilt by applying his home-grown calico-making technology to the production of chintz in India and exporting it back home. So it was only a matter of time before he grew immensely wealthy. It helped that he had married well – Sophia Elizabeth Auriol (fourteen years younger than him), the sister of Warren Hasting's secretary. This was in 1782.

John Prinsep was nothing if not a master integrator – forward, backward and sideways. He soon acquired the ships that he needed for his trading activities. By 1788, seventeen years from the time he set foot on Indian shores with not a penny to his name, he had amassed an enormous fortune of some £40,000. He decided it was time to head home.

He used a part of his substantial savings from India to buy a colossal frescoed mansion at 147 Leadenhall Street in London and with the rest set up Westminster Life Assurance Company, from which he would make his second big fortune. Already well entrenched in the political establishment, he soon became a London municipal councillor (1802-06) and then a member of parliament from Queenborough, Kent (1804-09).

By the time of his return to Britain, he already had three children. Between 1789 and 1803, he had eight more. Almost all of them seem to have been artistically gifted; all his sons, helped by the well-connected father, served in India; and all of them reached very important positions in their careers.

Unfortunately, following calamitous reverses in his insurance business, he lost most of his fortune and repaired to Bristol in south-west England. Three of his youngest sons spent their early years here, under conditions of some privations, living in an attic shielded by a cloth curtain and the three brothers sharing a trouser.

Subsequently, thanks to his connections, John took up position as high bailiff – a senior law enforcement official – in Southwark, London, from 1817 to 1824, and later as master of the Worshipful

Company of Skinners of London – a well-known livery company. He died in 1830, at the ripe age of eighty-four, leaving a rich legacy, if not riches, behind.

JAMES PRINSEP

James Prinsep, the protagonist of this chapter, was John's sixth son and ninth child, born in 1799. He did his early schooling in Clifton, a suburb of the port city of Bristol. With several older brothers and sisters at home, much of his education came from home tutoring. He showed early promise at detailed drawings, like many of his siblings. Mechanical and precise drawings, as well as designing mechanical devices, fascinated him. So he took up his studies in architecture under Augustus Pugin – an eminent architect, well known for his design of churches in England, Ireland and Australia in the Gothic revival style (he also designed the interior of the Palace of Westminster).

But James developed some eye problem, perhaps owing to the excessive strain of peering for long hours at detailed drawings, and his sight declined rapidly, making it impossible to continue his studies and a career in architecture. Fortunately, the problem was significantly corrected later.

His powerful father took to guiding his young son personally. He sent James to a well-known hospital to learn applied chemistry and had him intern at the Royal Mint of London under the assay master (the official who assesses the purity of gold or silver coins or the bullion at a mint). In 1819, John Prinsep despatched his nineteen-year-old son, accompanied by his brother Henry Thoby, older than James by seven years, to work in the assay department headed by Dr D.H. Wilson at the Calcutta Mint, established in 1757.

Within a year, Wilson transferred James to the Benares Mint, where he remained for the next decade. This move was considered highly unglamorous. Calcutta was the happening English city in the east and was the scene of action for anyone with promise. And yet, James chose to look at the bright side, finding opportunities in Benares where most would have found only weaknesses. He used his spare time away from the mint to show the beautiful side of India – its languages, antiquities and heritage – to the world through his writings and paintings. He instinctively fell in love with Benares, its many ghats, its temples, and its Hindustani music.

And when the mint was closed in 1830, he returned to Calcutta to the new mint as the deputy assay master under his old boss, Wilson. A year later, in 1831, he succeeded Wilson as the assay master of the mint, even though Wilson had been keen on another candidate. Wilson, a renowned Indologist himself, had resigned his position to join Oxford University to teach Sanskrit.

James married Harriet Sophia Aubert, daughter of a lieutenant-colonel of the Bengal army, in 1835. Two years later, they had their first child, a daughter – Eliza. He became seriously ill in 1838, returned to England and died in 1840. It is said that his intense mental activity while he was in weak health, probably led to a brain tumour.

He had suffered severe privations in his early life. His childhood was disrupted by poor eyesight, which in turn disrupted his early architectural career. In all, he spent about ten years in Benares and eight in Calcutta at the two mints. Nevertheless, James turned out to be one of the most multi-faceted personalities of colonial India, bordering on the genius.[i] He made significant impact in such diverse fields as 'civil engineering, geometry, mathematics, astronomy, natural sciences, anthropology, archaeological

---

[i] According to O.P. Kejariwal, Director, Nehru Memorial Library and author of *James Prinsep With James Prinsep and Benares* (Pilgrims Book House, New Delhi, 2009), 'If you draw a graph of human genius, James would head the list along with Leonardo da Vinci.'

disciplines, including epigraphy, and numismatics and history', in practically none of which he had any formal training.[2]

Let us take a closer look at some of the many facets he presented to the world in a professional life that spanned less than two decades.

JAMES THE ARCHITECT, AND BENARES

The old-world ghats of Benares caught James Prinsep's imagination like nothing else. An early riser, he would complete his paperwork by breakfast and then go on a beat around town. His attachment to Benares exceeded that of any veteran son of the soil. In his mere decade-long stay there, he contributed more to the city than anyone else we can think of, before or since. James had a keen and an enquiring mind and a flair for converting his ideas into reality. He used his mind and abilities to good effect for the city he had come to love – a love at first sight.

For starters, he computed the latitude and longitude of the ancient city through a detailed survey, through which he also produced an accurate map, capturing every single dwelling, on a scale of 8 inches to a mile. The map would eventually be lithographed in London in 1829.

He was the first ever to hold a comprehensive census survey. And he needed all his natural tenacity to do this. For example, holding a census survey posed serious challenges, given that the city had a huge floating population of pilgrims. How does one conduct a headcount of the resident population alone under the circumstances? Not only did Prinsep take on the challenge, he also conducted a survey of pilgrims in the peak pilgrimage season by deputing enumerators at five entry points and the many landing points in the city. He devised an ingenious method whereby the enumerators kept sacks full of pebbles and threw one pebble for each arrival into another bag, to be counted later.

Figure 1: The cantonment city of Bunarus, by James Prinsep, 1822.

He gave the city a drainage system that serves it even today. He designed a system of arched tunnels to drain the stagnant lakes of the city.

As a more or less trained architect, he built a stone bridge over the Karmanasa River – a tributary of the Ganga – over which the

Grand Trunk Road connecting the north of India to the south would pass. This was a bridge that had defeated bridge builders for well over a hundred years. However, the challenge of the bridge was perhaps more social than structural.

It arose from various superstitions and misplaced beliefs. For example, the river water was considered cursed and fatal to all mortals other than Brahmins. And the Brahmins weren't keen to allow a bridge to be built, the process of which could dispel the myth. But more importantly, there seems to have been a powerful lobby of inhabitants who ran a thriving business of transporting people on their backs across the river. A bridge would obviously hit their income. James managed these challenges, thanks to the overwhelming support he enjoyed among the locals. Once these were overcome, the structural challenge became a far more manageable one.

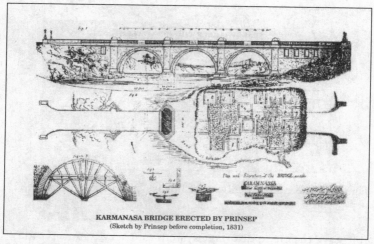

KARMANASA BRIDGE ERECTED BY PRINSEP
(Sketch by Prinsep before completion, 1831)

Figure 2: The Karmanasa bridge, designed and sketched by Prinsep.

He also designed a new mint building in the city as well as a church. At the same time, he paid attention to mending some of

Emperor Aurangzeb's minarets which were in a state of disrepair. Nor was this an easy task. The structures, with all their towers and spires, were extremely complex. When one of the old mosques tilted towards the river, with its fall into the river imminent, Prinsep took detailed note of the position of each brick of the structure so that when he restored the mosque, the sanctity of its original architecture was preserved faithfully.

JAMES THE ARTIST

Nowhere was his love for Benares more apparent than in his magnificent work, *Benares Illustrated* – a series of illustrations drawn by him. Their subjects included ancient monuments, astronomical themes, mechanical instruments, fossils and much besides. His eyesight properly restored, he brought to bear his old skill at detailed drawings to his passion for Benares. There were perhaps few winter afternoons when he wasn't seated on one of the many ghats of what he is fondly said to have referred to as 'our Ganga', capturing the scenes in his glorious drawings.

Figure 3: Kupuldhara Tulao, Benares, 1834,
as rendered by James Prinsep.

The drawings portray the beautiful Benares of the imperial times in timeless elegance of three-dimensional rendering, capturing the many plays of light and shade of the temples on the ghats. His works at the ghats, which include a number of water colours, were published between 1830 and 1834, titled *Benares Illustrated, in a Series of Drawings*. For this alone, he could easily be counted among the gifted geniuses of his age, even if he had done nothing else in his short life.

JAMES THE MECHANICALLY MINDED INNOVATOR

As if it was not versatile enough to be a gifted artist, engineer, numismatist, historian and philologist, James had a ready understanding of every kind of mechanical contraption there was. He never gave up on his childhood love of designing devises of his own. There was hardly a moment when his mind wasn't in overdrive. Among the more important of his improvements was to the balance. His version was the most accurate balance in the world at the time – so precise that it could measure a grain to 3/1000th degree of accuracy. In short, this balance could weigh a speck of dust.

He then picked up the barometer and devised an automatic compensator for temperature differences.[3] From here it was but a short step to come up with a contraption to measure rainfall within 0.005 inches and evaporation within 0.001 inches. He kept a meticulous meteorological register and would support anyone with barometers for furthering meteorological data collection.

If it's raining, can rust be far behind? His experiments on how to prevent rusting of iron surfaces were published in the *Journal of the Asiatic Society of Bengal* and presumably helped future scientists.[4]

He thought of a pyrometric device for the measurement of high temperatures. While he experimented with a series of calibrated mica slats, he finally settled on using a calibrated system of alloys of platinum, gold and silver, which melted at different temperatures. By noting the melting of the metals in a crucible, he proposed to calibrate the device. He worked out another design, which used the expansion of air inside a gold bulb for measuring temperature. In 1828, he published a paper in *The Philosophical Transactions of the Royal Society of London*, titled 'On the Measurement of High Temperatures'.[5]

He also worked on standardizing weights and measures and called for a uniform coinage along the lines of the new silver rupee minted by the East India Company.

Some sense of adventure has also been ascribed to him. When an aeronaut and a Frenchman, who had earlier made sixteen ascents in a giant balloon, passed through Calcutta 'for the purpose of astonishing the natives with the novel tomasha of a human being wafted out of sight into ethereal space' over the beautiful city on the banks of the Hooghly, he found himself challenged with the task of finding someone who knew how to make lighter-than-air gas.

While the attempt itself was hardly a resounding success for lack of preparedness and suitability of the site and so forth, some have suggested that Prinsep may have been the person to help the Frenchman with his search for a 'lighter-than-air gas'. However, there is little to support his involvement in the balloon episode in more formal references.[6]

JAMES THE NUMISMATIST

Returning to Calcutta after ten years in Benares, Prinsep found that the energy of the city, with its superior facilities in virtually everything, matched his own energy. He was even more empowered now that he was back with some of his well-placed brothers.

Numismatics competed for time with his many other preoccupations. As the assay master of a mint and a keen

Indologist, it should hardly be surprising that he had amassed a great variety of ancient Indian coins. It so happened that his mentor, Dr Wilson, had also been the secretary of the Asiatic Society; and so it fell to James to inherit that position as well.

Now there was a Captain James Herbert who had initiated a journal called *Gleanings in Science* in 1829. In 1830, he moved to Oudh as the royal astronomer to the king, leaving Prinsep to edit the journal, especially because he had been its primary contributor. As he was taking over as the secretary of the Asiatic Society of Bengal in 1832, Wilson suggested that the society should also take over *Gleanings in Science* and bring it out as a journal for the Asiatic Society. Thus Prinsep changed *Gleanings in Science* to the *Journal of the Asiatic Society* and became its first editor, involving himself neck-deep, or deeper, in its affairs. In the next six years or so, he would contribute articles in such diverse areas as numismatics, chemistry, mineralogy, Indian antiquities and so on.

With his keen interest in Indian antiquities, enriched by his experiences from his many travels, he would encourage his peers to report more and more on whatever they could find from all around the empire during their travels. These were times when the many surveys and construction activities were rapidly throwing up a number of new archaeological sites all over the empire.

His enthusiasm soon caught on. Before long, he was receiving a torrent of records, documents and reports on archaeological finds, ancient coins, old sculptures and ancient inscriptions – all of which became rich sources of articles for the society's journal. The society suddenly became a beehive of Indological activity. Contributions began to pour in from all over, the most significant of which were coins from across the length and breadth of India.

French General Jean Baptiste Ventura from Maharaja Ranjit Singh's court, who had excavated the Buddhist stupa of Manikyala in present-day Pakistan near Rawalpindi, sent his findings to the Asiatic Society. Similarly, another French officer from the same court presented a large cache of coins and inscriptions from Punjab to the society.

The unearthed coins obviously held rich information about Indian history and heritage but were largely uncategorized and ignored as they were incomprehensible. This was mainly because any one coin had too little lettering to provide a large enough sample to link any pattern of the script to the language it represented. For instance, the Brahmi script alone could represent Vedic, Sanskrit, Prakrit or Pali languages or several other South Asian languages. Or Kharosthi (closely related to the late Brahmi script) could represent Gandhari, Sanskrit or several other South Asian languages.

Prinsep applied himself to cracking the mysteries of these coins. His ever-sharp mind noticed that a large number of inscriptions and coins seemed distinctly to belong to particular scripts (Brahmi and Kharosthi) that bore little resemblance to the scripts on some other coins and inscriptions. He devoted ten years, or a quarter of his total life and nearly half of his adult life, to understanding the Brahmi script.

He assiduously read the works of his predecessors. He spent night after night poring over engravings on the ancient coins and other inscriptions without being able to make much sense of the epigraphic letterings on them. Slowly and steadily he stretched the boundaries of what had been understood of these inscriptions until then by his predecessors. His insight into philology and coins became sharper.

He studied coins from Bactria and Kushan (in present-day Afghanistan; his work relating to the coins from this region would be published by his brother Henry Thoby Prinsep in 1844). He worked out that the coins had been developed over three distinct stages: the punch-marked, the die-struck, and the moulded coins. Earlier, he had been of the view that coins were external to India. But soon he revised his opinion, figuring that punch-marked and moulded coins in gold and silver had ancient lineage in India. That is how he sorted out the punch-marked coins from the Gupta period.

In much of his work, he was ably assisted by another notable Briton, Sir Alexander Cunningham (about whom you will read more later). Cunningham shared James's passion for philology and archaeology and voluntarily assisted him, contributing to many of his findings.

JAMES THE PHILOLOGIST

The *Journal of the Asiatic Society* would turn out to be the best thing that had happened to Prinsep, given his love of numismatics and Indology. With the torrent of material and coins coming his way, he published a series of papers on numismatics between 1836 and 1838. It is said that no one ever died of hard work. Well, James may be an exception. He worked so relentlessly despite his increasingly indifferent health that he virtually worked himself to death.

It was in this phase of his life that he finally decoded the inscriptions on the rock edicts of ancient India. He looked deep into the Kharosthi script available on many inscriptions from the north-west of the Indian empire. And then he turned his attention to the Brahmi script.

The Brahmi script – a Dravidian script – had posed the biggest challenge until then to every scholar devoted to Indology. Even though much work had been done by various scholars to understand it, there were yet far too many gaps for it to be actually readable. Prinsep decided to find the bridge to close those gaps.

The many edicts found in the eastern part of India were in Magadhi – which used the Brahmi script – and frequently referred to a certain king by the name of Devanampriya Piyadasi. At first, Prinsep and others assumed that this was a Sri Lankan king.

However, among the material he received at the *Journal of the Asiatic Society* were some facsimiles of inscriptions in the Pali script, sent by one George Turnour, which referred to a certain Ashoka.

By piecing together the minute bits of the jigsaw puzzle slowly but accurately, Prinsep became convinced that King Piyadasi (Priyadarshi) was none other than Emperor Ashoka, whose inscriptions were found on many pillars from Delhi and Allahabad, going back to the third century BC. In time, these pillars would come to be known as the Ashoka Pillars.

By 1837, his keen understanding of these inscriptions helped him date various Indian dynasties, though his researches extended well beyond India – for instance, into Afghanistan and Greece as well. It was as if by cracking the Brahmi script, a huge block in the plumbing lines of Indian history had been unclogged in one go. Thanks to his keen insight and ability to see patterns across seemingly unrelated objects such as Buddhist stupas and coins of similar vintage, Prinsep managed to crack a number of ancient inscriptions, thus pushing Indian history back by a few centuries.

The Edicts of Ashoka

Now, the edicts of Ashoka hold a special place in Indian recorded history. They comprise a collection of thirty-three inscriptions, etched on a number of pillars, boulders and cave walls. Emperor Ashoka of the Mauryan dynasty, who reigned between 269 BC and 231 BC, is known to have commissioned them. The pillars, boulders and caves, representing the early evidence of the teachings of Buddhism, are scattered across the Indian subcontinent – from India to Bangladesh to Pakistan and Nepal. It was as if Ashoka had taken it upon himself to single-handedly spread the message of Buddhism across the length and breadth of the land.

The edicts inform us that Buddhism was carried by Ashoka as far as the Mediterranean, where he catalysed the creation of several Buddhist monuments. Most of the inscriptions would revolve around Ashoka's conversion to Buddhism, his efforts to spread Buddhism, his moral, social and religious edicts, and his animal welfare programme preaching abhorrence of violence in all respects. And today, if we know so much about Ashoka, we have James Prinsep to thank in a large measure.

The edicts proclaim Ashoka's dharma as a Buddhist. The inscriptions indicate that he wanted Buddhism to be his state religion. However, he was more focussed on its social and moral aspects rather than its superficial manifestations. He described himself as 'King Priya-darshi', meaning the loved one of the gods.

Seventy-five years after Prinsep's death, in 1915, a British gold-miner, C. Beadon, would uncover a rock in a little hamlet called Maski in the Raichur district of Karnataka. The inscription on this rock would reconfirm that King Piyadasi was Ashoka, endorsing Prinsep's work, if an endorsement was needed. A similar endorsement would come from another village, Gujarra, of Datia district in Madhya Pradesh. Here, the name Ashoka would be placed next to 'Devanampiyadasi'.

JAMES THE HUMANIST

James was not merely an all-round genius. He was a true humanist at heart. The divide-and-rule ruse the British employed in India was not lost on him. Within a short time of coming to India, he understood that the British shunned interactions with the great majority of Indians, restricting their communion to a select section of the Indian elite.

The unfair and often brutal treatment of the ordinary people for the smallest mistakes saddened him much, as many of his letters home – some of which can be found in the National Museum of

Scotland – would testify. His interactions with the common Indian would reflect this empathy.

END OF THE ROAD

Still in his thirties and hardly old, in 1838, an exhausted Prinsep decided to return to England. Though quite ill, he continued to work hard. He had enormous amounts of data and documents at his command, of which he had to make sense. He continued to work, continued to publish in diverse areas, and continued to remain sick.

Apart from regular attacks of headaches and fever, he developed some liver complications, leading him to return to Herefordshire in England's West Midlands region in 1838. The change of clime did not help, and his health continued to deteriorate, and he died at the age of forty from the 'softening of the brain', at his sister Sophia's residence at 31 Belgrave Square, London. It is perhaps this 'diagnosis' that connects the popular perception of his death to the overworking of his brain. John Forbes Royale, an eminent botanist, would immortalize the name of James Prinsep by naming a plant after him: Prinsepia is a genus of an Asian shrub of the rose family which bears cherry-like fruits.

His death triggered several memorials in India. The Asiatic Society commissioned a bust of James Prinsep to be sculpted by leading English portrait sculptor Francis Chantrey. As fate would have it, Chantrey died about a year after Prinsep so that the commission had to be completed by his protégé, Henry Weekes.

Calcutta also paid its homage by building the James Prinsep Memorial – an imposing Palladian Veranda designed by W. Fitzgerald – on the Hooghly's bank and naming the bank itself the Prinsep Ghat, which is overlooked today by Vidyasagar Setu, the second Hooghly bridge.

The truly human side of Prinsep was evident in how he related to the problems of the common people. The high rate of mortality in the local population troubled his conscience. Hordes of locals would die of malaria fever. The cause of malaria was considered to be mal-aria – that is, bad air that usually surrounds marshy and muddy surroundings, of which there was little dearth in the Benares of that time, as in the Benares (and much else of the country) of today.

Charles Alphonse Laveran, Patrick Manson and Ronald Ross – the trio whose collective work would ultimately link the female anopheles mosquito to malaria – were not yet born, but Prinsep perhaps intuitively linked mosquitoes at large with malaria and took it upon himself to drain the marshy and wet land masses of the city at his personal cost and with his own efforts. And remember, he was no British administrator of the civil services. He was the assay master of the mint. Such were the astounding results of his noble work that the people of Benares spontaneously gifted him a stretch of land as a token of their gratitude for arresting deaths from malaria.

And what do you think James Prinsep did with it? He deployed his engineering experience to perfectly level it to form a dry and non-flooding ground and returned it to the people of Benares for building a bazar. And this when Prinsep was actually poor himself, earning a very modest salary from an uncertain job.

Not only did James have the highest work ethics, he also had a deep sense of family honour. His brother Thomas Prinsep had been in charge of surveying the Sunderbans. When Thomas accidentally died after falling off a horse, James took it upon himself to complete his brother's work, to protect the family name. He cut channels through the marshy water body, dividing it into canals and reclaimed islands.

5

The Grand Visionary

*Arthur Thomas Cotton: The Man Who
Dammed India*

1803–1899

THE GRAND ANICUT, ALSO known as the Kallanai, is an ancient
dam of uncut stone built on the Kaveri River in Tamil Nadu. It
is 1,080 feet long and 60 feet wide, and its purpose was to divert
the water across the fertile delta region for irrigation via canals.
The area irrigated by the ancient irrigation network of which the
dam was the centrepiece was 69,000 acres (or 280 sq km). This
was an impressive structure by any account. And this one, with
its origins in the first century AD, was built by Karikala Chola, a
great Tamil king.

There was one man whose name would get intimately
associated with this region, who was responsible for building
on this achievement of ancient India and increasing the irrigated

area from 69,000 acres to about 10,00,000 acres (4,000 sq km) in his lifetime. A hundred years after all the additions to the dam, it remains in excellent shape and provides inspiration to many an engineer even today.

The man behind this and a host of other impressive projects was one of the all-time great engineers of the British Empire, who, in 1858 – nearly a century and a half ago – dared to dream of an ambitious project to link all the major Indian rivers to exploit the full irrigation and navigational potential in the country – an infrastructure project we quake to contemplate even today.

He spent much of his long life trying to realize his dreams, only to be thwarted by the then Madras government. Consequently, his achievements, though extraordinary by any yardstick, fell short of his own tall dreams. He did, however, manage to build a dam across the Kollidam – a major distributary of the Kaveri – in the 19th century. This work on the Kollidam would pave the way for some great projects on the Godavari and Krishna river systems.

His dam on the Godavari, with channels, embankments, and roads across the Godavari delta, would enrich Andhra Pradesh enormously, especially the Konaseema area, that is, the delta between the East and West Godavari districts. The same man prepared plans for the Visakhapatnam port. Unfortunately, his plans to connect all the canals and rivers in Odisha to save the region from its perennial drought did not take shape. He was knighted in 1861 and later, in 1877, decorated with the honour of the Knight Commander of Supreme India.

Who was this man, also known as Bhageeratha both in Andhra Pradesh and Tamil Nadu, who has more than 3,000 statues of him installed all over East and West Godavari, and for whom to this day farmers of Konaseema do tharpanam – offering of water mixed with gingelly to dead ancestors – by chanting a shloka in his name? What led to his near-deification in certain parts of India? What is the story of his great achievements? Read on.

COTTONREDDYPALEM

Cottonreddypalem, as in cotton-reddy-palem, in the West Godavari district of Andhra Pradesh, is not a cotton-growing area. In fact, it has nothing to do with cotton. It is a different matter that Cotton is a household name in this region, and generations of males have some derivative of Cotton in their names, even if the knighted general, Sir Arthur Cotton, our hero, does not necessarily ring a bell in the minds of an average Indian today outside the Godavari belt.

Across the Godavari, 10 km downstream from the city of Rajahmundry and 80 km from the coast, is the little township of Dowleswaram or Dowlaiswaram or Dhavaleswaram, depending on how you like to spell it. The town is home to many temples and the Dowleswaram Barrage. The structure is built on the last possible stretch of the river, just before it splits into two distributaries – Gautami and Vasishta. Between the two, which further split into several branches and empty into the Bay of Bengal, is the Godavari central delta. The towns of Dowleswaram and Cottonreddypalem are a stone's throw from the point where the festival of Pushkaram is held every twelve years – like the Kumbh mela.

About two and a half centuries ago, a young engineer brought his energies and intellect to bear on reconciling the districts of Godavari ravaged by famines and cyclones with the fact that the big river passing through it emptied 80 per cent of its water during the rainy season into the ocean year after year. He felt that the water emptying into the ocean could be harnessed for the prosperity of the region. The man was Arthur Thomas Cotton.

ARTHUR THOMAS COTTON

Arthur was born in Woodcote, a small and simple village at the highest point in the Southern Chilterns after Nuffield in Southern Oxfordshire, England, on 15 May 1803. He was the tenth of the eleven children of Henry Calveley Cotton, himself the tenth son of Sir Lynch Cotton (the fourth holder of a baronetcy created in 1677 in favour of Sir Robert Cotton, a member of parliament from Cheshire), and Matilda, daughter and heiress of John Lockwood of Dews Hall, Essex. Thus the family was of some antiquity. The family was eminent and the boys – at least seven of them – grew up to uphold that eminence through their varied careers. Sir Arthur Cotton would grow up to be a most distinguished engineer, but by no means the only distinguished member of his family.

Arthur's future was evident in his childhood itself. He was on a walk with his mother and one of his sisters when they happened to notice a strange hue in the water in a gutter. The next moment, the mother and sister found little Arthur missing. Hours later when he surfaced at home, he informed them of the source of the red colour in the gutter water – a dye factory some distance away.[1]

Place some bread on his plate and a glass of milk, he would sooner play dams and canals with the two rather than eat his bread and drink his milk. His brothers would note that once when they were out on a rainy day, little Arthur kept falling behind. The reason, it turned out, was that he was busily chalking canals on the road with his stick. He was absorbed in linking different rain puddles through a system of networking canals.

In 1818, at the age of fifteen, Arthur was sent to the Military Academy at Addiscombe in Surrey – the counterpart of the Royal Military Academy at Woolwich, the predecessor of the Royal Military Academy, Sandhurst – the preeminent institution of choice for a military career for the wealthy. This was the facility where cadets for the artillery and engineering service of the East Indian Company were traditionally trained. Arthur went through the course gloriously.

Even 200 years ago, there was concern 'that a very large number of younger persons are not willing to work hard. They are anxious to do, in return for their pay, as little as they can.'[2] But Arthur gave no cause for concern to his seniors at school or at home. Such was his diligence that his superiors appointed him to the Royal Engineers even without an examination in 1819 when he was not yet seventeen.

For starters, in January 1820, he was posted to the Ordnance Survey in Wales, Chatham. The youngster evidently showed glimpses of his potential as he won high praise for his excellence at work. In a region with few roads and wild expanses, he walked all over the countryside surveying the region. His report attracted considerable attention.

The very next year, barely eighteen, he was posted to India. He boarded the ship for India in May 1821 and arrived in unfamiliar Madras (present-day Chennai) in September after a four-month voyage and reported to the chief engineer of Madras Presidency.

Arthur spent his first year trying to get to grips with his assignment. The year after, he was appointed assistant engineer to the superintending engineer, Captain J. Fullerton, of the tank department in the southern division of the presidency.

There is a legend associated with his life which pertains to about this time. According to it, Arthur was one of three officers being interviewed for the position of the engineer. They were all told to have a good night's sleep and to report the next morning. Apparently, Arthur had a rather fitful sleep that night. Next morning, they were asked if they had had a good night's sleep. While two of the officers perfunctorily stated that they did, Arthur said that he had found sleep difficult. At one point in the night, not quite happy with his orientation – he thought one of the cot's legs a tad too high – he had investigated this and found a pound coin underneath. Needless to say, he got the job.

One of his early assignments in 1822 was the prestigious survey of the Paumben Pass, the narrow gully amidst rocks between India and Ceylon (present-day Sri Lanka) – what is called the Adam's

Bridge. Soon, in 1923, his preliminary spade work led to large ships being able to pass through the chasm and brought down the travel time around the Indian peninsula.

The Paumben Pass survey done, between 1822 and 1824, the young officer was called to supervise repairs of tanks in the districts of Coimbatore, Madura (Madurai), Tinnevelly (Tirunelveli), Trichinopoly (Tiruchirappalli) and Tanjore (Thanjavur). These were the districts where Arthur learnt much about harnessing water, its storage and distribution – work that would lay the foundations of greater things to come.

The first Burma war was looming on the horizon. Arthur volunteered to be drafted. He spent the next two years in Burma (Myanmar), aboard patrolling gunboats, and was involved in the storming of the fortresses of Tavoy (Dawei) and Mergui (Myeik) in the Tanesserin region, with the defence of Rangoon (Yangon) and assault on the stockades of Kakien. Here, he virtually abandoned his supporting role as an engineer and played the infantry role, leading his troops against no less than seven forts and stockades.

The Burmese campaign over, the young lieutenant was sailing back to Madras. Sitting on the deck of his gently bobbing ship, he was gazing lazily at the bright skies illuminated by a million twinkling stars, with a gentle breeze kissing his cheeks, and mused: 'Who made these worlds? Upon whose handiwork am I gazing now? It is the work of God, the great Creator.'

Thus came religion to the young officer, who had not been religious at all till then, and he actually went down into the living quarters and asked for a copy of the Bible. This would stay with him for his lifetime and remain his conscience.

Upon reaching Madras, he was appointed as acting superintendent engineer of the central division of the tank department. He was soon confirmed in this position. His Burmese sojourn brought him down with a severe bout of lung fever and infection. As soon as he recovered, he was dispatched to Paumben

Pass once again for some fine-tuning of the surveys. There was virtually no money for any actual work on the pass. Arthur used a modest budget of less than £400 effectively to deepen the pass by another two or three feet.

It was 1827 and Lieutenant Cotton, all of twenty-four, had put in eight years of outstanding service and was now promoted to Captain.

THE GRAND ANICUT OF KAVERI

The Kaveri has always been a temperamental river through history. A highly revered river in the south of India, it is known to have changed its course frequently on account of the large amounts of silt it carries. In addition to this moodiness of its trajectory, the river is known to silt up its surroundings with frequent floods, rendering them uncultivable.

As early as the second century BC, King Karikalan of the Chola dynasty had taken it upon himself to address the problem. His answer was the semi-circular Grand Anicut or Kallanai – a massive dam of uncut stones and lime and sand mix. This is probably the oldest dam-cum-irrigation structure in the world still in use.

The British had realized that agriculture in the Kaveri delta – that is Thanjavur and its adjoining regions – was in serious trouble. This was because the moody Kaveri was threatening to change its course and join the Coleroon (or Kollidum) – its own distributary – a little upstream from Tiruchirappalli, thus jeopardizing the fertile delta. Perhaps it was with this very danger in mind that the government had acquired the Grand Anicut and the surrounding deltas just around the turn of the century in 1801. They appointed Captain James Lilliman Caldwell, a military engineer, to study the Kaveri and develop irrigation in the delta region. He raised the dam stones to a height of 0.69 metre in order to increase the capacity of the dam.

However, for the next three decades, the British kept their fingers crossed and tried to make do with patchwork on the Grand Anicut. They raised its height periodically so as to channel as much Kaveri waters into the canals as possible, though this was not an answer to the fundamental problem of the river changing its course. A more permanent solution was needed, and needed urgently.

CAPTAIN COTTON

Captain Cotton was now provided an opportunity that would define his destiny. He was given additional charge of the Kaveri's irrigation network, which in fact fell under the southern division. Cotton, now deeply religious, was far more sensitive to people's suffering than the British government, whose chief concern was probably the depleting tax collection from the impoverished region of the Kaveri delta.

His heart beat for the poor farmers who were getting poorer by the season. His keenness to help them went beyond the call of duty. He launched himself headlong into an understanding of the Kaveri and the Grand Anicut and their place in the socio-economic well-being of the local inhabitants there.

Interestingly, the 'Grand' Anicut was largely a structure of garbage, mud, stones and logs of wood, held in place by a lime-bound surface. And even more interestingly, this discovery was made not by Cotton but by the youngest of the Cotton brothers – Frederick – who was also working in Madras as an engineer. The discovery was made in the course of his cutting sluices into the anicut in order to drain the accumulated silt from behind the weir.

That this simple but ingenious structure of King Karikalan's engineers should have withstood the test of time for over two millennia came as a revelation to the Cotton brothers. Clearly, evidence of India's 'frugal engineering' – the term in vogue today – was already in existence. The brothers were prompted to coin the term 'Madras (or cheap) School of Engineering' to connote inexpensive engineering, and they founded the School of Indian Hydraulic Engineering.

'Why invest in unnecessarily massive structures? After all, what is good engineering but economy!' Frederick is reported to have exclaimed.[3] The Cotton brothers were no longer playing with water puddles. Arthur was living out his childhood dreams in the 1830s.

The Grand Anicut had already provided Arthur more than two thousand years' worth of understanding of barrage building and knowledge about taming the Kaveri. Working closely with his brother, he borrowed liberally from the minimalist design of the Grand Anicut in order to build another one on the Coleroon (or Kollidum) just below where it departed from the Kaveri.

This structure stands even today as an eloquent testimony of a leading English engineer paying homage to the ancient Indian genius of engineering.

Arthur's genius also stretched to material sourcing. He sourced all the granite required for the barrage from within the boundary wall of a nearby disused ancient temple, with due permission from the priests.

Another barrage on the Kollidum was simultaneously built further downstream, about 70 km from the first. It helped irrigate another 1,65,000 acres of land. The inhabitants of the region would forever be grateful to the great engineer for the barrages – particularly the upper one.

Time was flying. By 1838, he had ensured that Thanjavur was the richest region of the Madras Presidency and returned the highest revenue.

In 1841, at the ripe age of thirty-eight, Arthur finally found the time to marry. His wife was Elizabeth Learmonth, daughter of Thomas Livingstone Learmonth. They had two children, Elizabeth Reid (1842), who would be Lady Hope in due course, and Alfred (1850), who would grow up to be Major Alfred Fox Cotton.

THE GODAVARI ANICUT OR THE COTTON BARRAGE

Godavari delta was witnessing its worst drought in years. From a population of 7.4 lakh, the population of Rajahmundry was down to 5.6 lakh during the 1830s. According to one report, such was the death toll in the famine that a strong posse of police were engaged in 'collecting the dead and throwing them into a huge pit … [and yet could not] keep the ground clear'.

Droughts in the Godavari belt were a periodic feature. And with every drought, apart from wide-scale death, tax collection took a serious beating. This probably was a matter of greater concern to the British than the death toll. The falling tax revenue was perhaps as much on account of the famine as large land owners going steadily bankrupt. Their bankruptcy in turn was perhaps as much on account of their own profligate lifestyles as the British closing down cloth-buying centres. The closure of these centres in turn was perhaps due to the disruption in the growing of cotton by the land owners because of the disregard of the irrigation canals emanating from the Godavari. The fact was that the loss in tax revenue pinched the government where it hurt most.

The British government was keen to address the problem and appointed one Henry Montgomery – a former collector of Thanjavur – to investigate the delta's potential in detail. Understandably, he was aware of the excellent work done by Arthur Cotton and his contributions to the irrigation systems of the region. Cotton was at that time flirting with his first and the only railway project in India – a short line around Madras. He was also engaged in studying the plans for developing a port in Visakhapatnam and had built a church there. Montgomery sought him out to study the Godavari belt and come up with a report.

Travelling through the famine-struck districts of the Godavari basin, Cotton became intimately familiar with the suffering of the famished masses. This genuinely distressed him. And when he observed the bulk of the Godavari's vast supply of water just running into the sea while the entire region remained starved of water, he could see plainly that the answer to the problems of the masses was to tame the mighty Godavari – a river system lesser only than the Gangetic and the Indus river systems. His prescription for the people's misery was to build a barrage on the Godavari.

Not surprisingly, Cotton didn't stop at a perfunctory report. He presented a detailed plan to harness the Godavari. His plan entailed building a sprawling barrage spanning the east and west of the district – what would come to be known as the Cotton Barrage, or Godavari Anicut, at Dowleswaram.

So excited was he with the idea that in 1847 he commenced the construction without waiting for authorization from his superiors. His moral uprightness and tendency to speak his mind had earned him more detractors than friends, and professional jealousies can be really petty. He was disliked by his superiors because of his compassion for Indians. As a consequence, he was nearly impeached and dismissed for his unauthorized construction. After all, he was a mere executive engineer.

Arthur remained forever impatient with the sluggish pace of the Indo-British bureaucracy, and the bureaucracy constantly remained on the lookout to irritate him. Nor was this the end of his troubled association with the barrage.

The construction of the barrage on the Godavari commenced. But no sooner had it begun than he fell ill in 1848 and left for Australia for convalescence. He was away for nearly a year, leaving one Captain Orr to oversee the operations. Returning in 1850, promoted as a colonel now, he immersed himself deeply in the construction work to make up for lost time. He used the highest quality of lime, wood and stone available locally. He pressed about 1,500 workers to work round the clock to complete the 3.6 km barrage, comprising four sections and straddling the East and

West Godavari districts. He managed to complete the project in a record time of five years.

Even by today's standards, that must be considered a remarkable feat.

And what is more, he also completed the work on the Gannavaram aqueduct at the same time. The huge flow of water arrested from flowing into the sea was now channelled through three canals – one each for the eastern, western and central deltas, irrigating the surrounding districts as never before.

Referring to the Godavari, he made a pithy observation in 1856: 'The river must be restrained from wandering ... and all its branches must be provided with artificial embankments to protect the country from being flooded ... It is necessary, by artificial means, to keep the water constantly at a level which shall command the country, and also by a multitude of channels to lead it to every acre of land ... The system of works now in progress in the Delta of the Godavery are intended to embrace these four objects, viz – to restrain the river; to preserve the land from floods; to supply it constantly with water; and to pervade the tract thoroughly with means of very cheap transit.'[4]

Thanks to Cotton's energy and enterprise, a wasteland was transformed into the rice bowl of India virtually overnight. From a highly uncertain supply of water, the region now acquired a round-the-year supply, turning a large parched and barren land mass into a most fertile one. If only Cotton had been given a freer hand, if only he had not been impeded by petty bureaucratic hurdles, he might well have connected Godavari and Krishna in the same vein and changed the fate of the region forever. And had he done so, there was no reason why he could not have given shape to his dream of linking all the major rivers of India.

Cotton estimated the life of the barrage he had built at a hundred years. He did not know that maintenance of the barrage would always remain neglected. Theoretically, this ought to reduce the estimated longevity. And yet, so outstanding was the quality of Cotton's work that the barrage continued to function perfectly for nearly 130 years and it was only some time in the 1980s that some much-needed repairs were carried out, giving the anicut another lease of life.[5] Thus the good old barrage continues to serve the coastal Andhra region with renewed vigour, even if there were accounts of some damage to it reported by the *Hindu* in 2012.[6]

AFTER THE GODAVARI ANICUT

Having finished the magnificent project, Cotton turned to building an aqueduct on the Kistna (Krishna). The project was approved just as the Godavari barrage was nearing completion and completed by other officers in 1855.

Of his work post-anicut, Cotton would observe, 'The revenue of the Delta, including that part that is in Masulipatnam, has increased about 60,000 Pounds ... (and) the amount of money re-circulated in the district has increased to 100,000 Pounds, above the average in years preceding the works; the internal traffic is now estimated at 180,000 tons carried thirty miles ...'[7]

Though nearing superannuation, in 1858, Cotton energetically mobilized much-needed investments for the large-scale irrigation projects in a bid to privatize irrigation systems, especially as the government was unwilling to cough up the funds required. He spawned the Madras Irrigation Company (MIC) in 1858 with the object of concentrating on the Tungabhadra river system.

Cotton was nearing the end of his career. He finally retired in 1860. For his outstanding contributions to the Indian subcontinent, he was knighted in 1861. Sir Arthur Thomas Cotton left for England soon after to settle down in the little market town of Dorking a little south of London. However, irrigation was never far from his mind. He returned to India the very year after his retirement and kept returning time and again to advise British India on various irrigation projects. He spent several of his retirement years pottering around with sundry gardening experiments, developing better tricycles, and penning Arabic primers for the church.

As late as 1873, he proposed yet another reservoir upstream of the Krishna. His unorthodox proposal was to explode a million pounds of dynamite to create a huge rock mass spanning a quarter of a mile across the river. In his opinion, the ensuing irrigation would enable a second crop in the year for the region – a winter crop following the conventional monsoon crop.

Unfortunately, the Madras government considered the proposal eccentric and ridiculed him for good measure. Cotton, in turn, reacted by proposing another, far more audacious scheme. The proposal, if accepted, would link *all* the major rivers in the country through a network of canals that would irrigate the whole of India. His simple argument was, 'There is not a single acre of land in Bengal, in all of India, or in the whole world, that would not be more productive if irrigated at one time and drained at another.'[8] His other reason for connecting the rivers was to provide the subcontinent with a navigation system that would be a viable alternative to the railways. The entire project would cost the exchequer 50 million pound sterling (or about $300 billion in today's money – give or take).

The proposal would do a lot of damage to his reputation.

The Final Days

Unfortunately for Cotton, his brush-offs with the government were far from over. In fact, the Godavari barrage came back to haunt him. In 1878 – a year after he had been decorated as the Knight Commander of Supreme India – at seventy-five, he was asked to appear before the House of Commons to defend his proposal to build the barrage. In a letter to the secretary of state, he is reported to have written, 'My Lord, one day's flow in the Godavari during high floods is equal to one whole year's flow in the Thames ...'

This was followed up by yet another hearing before a parliamentary committee, where he was taken to task for his 100-foot-high and 8,000-foot-long dam or the 'Great Equalizing Reservoir' on the Tungabhadra – a distributary of the Krishna. This dam or reservoir was expected to irrigate another 1 million acres.

It may be an irony of history that both these dams – on the Krishna and Tungabhadra – were eventually built, albeit in the post-British era. The dam on the Krishna today is the Nagarjuna Sagar Dam – 400 feet tall and 5,000 feet long. The work on this dam commenced in 1956 and completed in 1967, when it ranked as the world's largest masonry dam. The Tungabhadra dam is built a few hundred kilometres upstream at Hospet. Evidently, the projects envisaged by the great Cotton will be hard to beat even today.

Cotton spent his last years preaching the Bible and experimenting with cultivating new strains of wheat. A deeply religious man, a great engineer and a genuine friend of India and its people, particularly farmers, Sir Arthur Thomas Cotton breathed his last at the ripe old age of ninety-six in July 1899.

On 23 November 2009, the *Hindu* reported that an Andhra Pradesh team, after some 'hectic efforts', had located the grave of Sir Arthur Thomas Cotton in a cemetery in Dorking. The tombstone's etching referred to him as 'Irrigation Cotton involved in construction of large scale irrigation projects, dams, aqueducts, bridges and canals in India'. It is understood that the Telugu Association of London has taken up the renovation of his tomb.[i]

---

[i] Alongside that of Sir Cotton was also located the tombstone of C.P. Brown, another Englishman, who contributed much to Telugu literature, including the first Telugu-to-English dictionary. The Telugu Association took up the renovation of his tomb as well.

CONTROVERSIAL LEGACY

Sir Cotton had started addressing the problems of severe water scarcity of India a good 150 years ahead of its time. Little wonder that he is celebrated as Bhageeratha – the mythological prince who is considered the primary mover for fetching the Ganga down to Earth from the heavens.

As recently as 15 May 2009, his 206th birthday was celebrated in the chambers of the irrigation minister of Andhra Pradesh at the state secretariat in Hyderabad. According to reports, the minister cut a cake and recounted the significant contributions made by Sir Cotton to the state, particularly in the form of the Godavari Anicut.

On the same occasion the previous year, the online edition of the *Hindu* reported that a farmer had offered 'abhishekam' with milk to a bronze statue of Sir Cotton and said, 'Now, we see [such abundance of water]. But for the engineering prowess of Sir Arthur Cotton, this region would have been in the grip of drought.'

According to a foreword in the 1987 reprint of the monograph *The Engineering Works of the Godavari Delta* by George T. Walch: 'The magnitude of work, the quickness of execution and the productivity of engineers working in the 1850s can best be realised when juxtaposed with similar works executed after technological advances, mechanisation, modern management practices and improved communication facilities ...'

Much of the literature available on Sir Cotton is unequivocal about his contributions. And yet, no great man is truly great unless he has his share of detractors. Sir Cotton may have been long gone, but Uma Maheshwari – a freelance journalist based in Hyderabad, working on tribal land dispossession in the Polavaram project – criticized his work in June 2009 (India Together, an online forum).

She picked a bone with him for taming what 'we today call ecological (natural) flows' and for having contributed to 'economic exploitation to maximize profits'. She accused him of having 'changed the traditional cropping patterns and methods of irrigation'. Under the title 'The Empire Flows Again', she rued the fact that 'within a month of the Congress government being re-elected in Andhra Pradesh, its irrigation minister has announced that the government seeks "national" (project) status for five irrigation projects related to Godavari waters.'

Her lament was expressed thus: 'More than a hundred years later, not only is his legacy of exploiting the river alive in the form of numerous projects that are ongoing, even his unfulfilled dreams of adding private exploitation to publicly funded ones are close at hand!'[9] Perhaps this scathing bit of criticism arose from the unethical practices that the East India Irrigation and Canal Company, a public-private partnership venture promoted by Sir Cotton, was reported to have adopted under his oversight of the company.

While one may be free to vent anger upon Sir Cotton, it should be remembered that the entire ecological debate was probably unheard of 150 years ago. To blame Cotton for wanting to 'tame' the Godavari's waters and use it for the irrigation of the region sounds preposterous. And yet, to his credit, Cotton paid his tribute to ecological considerations when he used a minimalist design for the barrage on the Kollidum, mimicking the 2,000-year-old design of the Grand Anicut of Kaveri. Also, the region served by him stands testimony to the fact that the benefits of his acts have far outweighed their costs, whatever they may have been.

As for causing changes in the crop pattern of the region, the crop growers themselves have never complained. On the contrary, they bask in the glory of being the rice bowl of India. It would be strange to let a famished people keep tilling fallow land for lack of irrigation merely to favour natural crop patterns. After all, what is a *natural* crop pattern? At one level, isn't cropping itself an 'unnatural' process, which, like technology, must constantly evolve? Crop patterns mean something only if one can grow substantial crop. Fallow and unirrigated land produces nothing.

It is nobody's case that the British government built the irrigation projects solely to allay the sufferings of Indian subjects. Of course, their primary motivation was tax revenue. However, even for a non-colonial government, a project involving large expenditure that does not bring about the well-being of the people and thus does not enhance the government's tax revenue can hardly be viable. In this sense, the fact that Cotton conceived of a project that helped increase tax revenue even as it gave immense benefit to the farmers can hardly be held against the great man.

Elizabeth Cotton, his daughter and an evangelist better known as Lady Hope, writes of her father that there was 'not an individual in the province who did not consider the upper anicut the greatest blessing that had ever been conferred upon it'.[10] According to one engineer from Bengal, 'The permanent prosperity of Tanjore [is] without question to be attributed in large measure to that first bold step taken by Colonel Cotton, in the construction of the upper Coleroon Dam, under circumstances of great difficulty, with restricted means, against much opposition, and with heavy personal responsibilities.'[11]

Sir Cotton has always been a recognized and larger-than-life hero for the coastal belt of southern India, especially Andhra Pradesh. His name is sacred for the farmers in the Godavari and Thanjavur belts. He remains a beacon for irrigation engineers in India even today as they take up many of the projects that he had already dreamt of, envisioned and planned, but unfortunately, thanks to a sluggish colonial bureaucracy, could not undertake.

6

Bringing Tea to Darjeeling

Dr Archibald Campbell: The Occasional Botanist

1805–1875

AS WITH MANY EVENTS historical, we rely on Goscinny and Uderzo, chroniclers of the exploits of Asterix, the famous comic book character, to give us accurate information. In the year 50 BC, they inform us,[i] exotic herbs that Getafix the Druid had sourced from 'faraway barbaric lands' found their way into an Englishman's cup of hot water, and the concoction soon became the national drink. By 1800 AD, tea was England's principal import from China. China knew this, and fiercely guarded the secrets of tea cultivation, successfully creating a monopoly. Many intrepid souls tried to smuggle leaves out of China at great personal risk, maybe even losing their lives in the process.

---

[i] See *Asterix in Britain*

One man did get some seedlings and planted them in Assam, but then, who knew how to make tea from plants? Soon, the British were not able to afford the extortionate market prices that the Chinese were charging and had to find other sources of tea. As it turned out, at least one of these sources turned out to be our Darjeeling, and this is the story of the man who made it happen.

Before the East India Company entered the area, Darjeeling was under the dominion of the Raja of Sikkim, sandwiched between Nepal and Bhutan and coveted by both. The raja's armies were no match for the neighbouring forces, and so he struck a deal with the British for his protection. Gorkhas from the west would make constant forays into the land that was once theirs, as would belligerent tribes from Bhutan – not to forget the occasional Tibetan incursions from the north.

In Sikkim itself, there were multiple tribes – the Lepchas, Moormis, Limboos and Mechis – which all spoke different languages, and although comparatively peace-loving, they had their own differences. They did have something in common, though: a high regard for a kind doctor named Archibald Campbell.

EARLY LIFE AND CAREER

Archibald Campbell was born on 20 April 1805 in Islay, a remote spot in the Scottish Inner Hebrides chain of islands. His father, also Archibald Campbell, Esq., was a whisky distiller, and his mother's name was Helen. Little is known about his early life, save for the fact that he studied at Glasgow University and then the University of Edinburgh from 1824 to 1827 and obtained a doctor of medicine degree.

Soon after graduating, Campbell was appointed an assistant surgeon in the services of the East India Company in 1827, and in 1828 he joined the horse artillery at Meerut that comprised all of six men. He served there for four years, but his health suffered because of the extreme heat combined with the damp conditions in the hospital barracks. At this stage, he moved to Landour near Mussoorie, where his health continued to worsen.

On his request, he was transferred to Kathmandu in 1832 to serve on the staff of the British Resident, Brian Houghton Hodgson. This turned out to be a lucky break for Archibald, because Hodgson was one of the foremost oriental scholars and naturalists of the time, an expert on the culture of Nepal, a collector of Sanskrit manuscripts and a keen naturalist whose influence would have a profound impact on Campbell's future career.

Hodgson had been involved in the study of cis- and trans-Himalayan tribes and the geology of Nepal and Tibet when Campbell arrived. Drawn to the nature of the study, he volunteered to assist Hodgson. Within a year, he had absorbed so much about the indigenous tribes of the Himalayas that Hodgson elevated him to the post of assistant resident. This might seem like a strange elevation for a surgeon, but from Hodgson's point of view, understanding the tribal people and their culture was vital for effective administration. Additionally, Hodgson's health was failing and it was Campbell he trusted most to continue his policy of development through an understanding of the local communities.

The Procurement of Darjeeling

Darjeeling derives its name from the Nepalese words 'dorje', meaning thunderbolt, and 'ling', meaning land. In the early 1830s, this was a sparsely populated region, mostly consisting of indigenous tribes which followed a hunter-gatherer lifestyle and occasionally practised slash-and-burn agriculture. When the British first eyed this place, it was almost entirely covered by forests and populated by not more than an estimated hundred people of the Lepcha tribe.[1]

The climate was pleasant, not unlike the cool ambience of the

British Isles, and definitely very different from the heat and dust
of the plains of the rest of India. It seemed like the ideal place
for the establishment of a 'sanatorium' where fatigued East India
Company officers beset by tropical diseases could recuperate, not
to mention get over some homesickness as well. In 1835, Captain
George Alymer Lloyd negotiated a lease for Darjeeling from the
Raja of Sikkim for an annual rent of Rs 3,000 (raised to Rs 6,000
in 1841. This, however, was not for the whole of present-day
Darjeeling but a narrow enclave about 30 miles long and 6 miles
wide.). The grant deed read:

> 'The Governor-General having expressed his desire for the
> possession of the hills of Darjeeling on account of its cool climate,
> for the purpose of enabling the servants of his Government,
> suffering from sickness, to avail themselves of its advantages, I
> the Sikkimputtee Rajah, out of friendship for the said Governor-
> General, hereby present Darjeeling to the East India, that is, all
> the land south of the Great Runjeet river, east of the Balasur,
> Kahail and Little Runjeet rivers, and west of the Rungpo and
> Mahanadi rivers.'[2]

The raja thought that this was a good deal, because, for him,
this was just a piece of forested mountain land, and moreover,
given the British presence, the Gorkhas would think twice before
making aggressive incursions into Sikkim.

In 1840, Dr Campbell was transferred from Kathmandu to
Darjeeling, vested with full civil charge of the new settlement. It was
a delicate task, as it involved maintaining good diplomatic relations
with all the neighbouring volatile kingdoms. He proceeded in a
manner he knew best – by *learning* all about them.

By the time he was finished, he had published no less than
forty papers (in the Journal of the Agricultural and Horticultural
Society of India) on the people, geography and meteorology –

ranging across such varied subjects as 'Musical Instruments of the Nipalese', 'Barometrical and Thermometrical Observations at Cathmandoo', 'Proboscis of the Elephant', 'Origin and Language of the Limboos', 'Arts of Weaving, Spinning and Dyeing in Nipal' and 'Observations of Goitre in Animals as It Occurs in Nipal'.

During this time (he was just thirty-five years of age), he was entrusted with negotiating a number of border disputes, all of which were settled satisfactorily at that time, speaking volumes for the regard that these otherwise irreconcilable tribes shared for the good doctor. This was recognized by the then governor-general, Lord Auckland, who observed in a public communication that British presence in Darjeeling was possible mainly 'by means of [Dr Campbell's] medical skills and kindness'.[3]

THE FIRST TEA GARDEN

The search for tea in India actually goes back a couple of decades more. In the early 1820s, Scottish brothers Robert and Charles Bruce found themselves serving in Assam – Robert as an army major and the younger Charles as a gunboat commander of the British navy. They were fighting the Burmese for control over the region. Robert had been in Assam for a while before his younger brother joined him – after a rather adventurous stint in the Napoleonic wars, having been captured by the French Army and taken prisoner.

The year was 1823, and the brothers who had been away from home for too long had heard about an Assamese beverage brewed from dried leaves that sounded similar to their favourite drink. The elder Bruce, Robert, decided to explore this further. He made friends with the chief of the Singhpo – an indigenous Assamese tribe – and had himself invited to his house, where he was served an amber liquid that closely resembled what he used to drink every evening back home. As a parting gift, he received several saplings that he planted in various regions of Assam.

Unfortunately, he died soon after, but Charles continued to care for the plants. He sent a few of them to be examined by experts at the Calcutta Botanical Gardens, where they were declared an inferior quality of tea, but unfit for regular tea production. And so the tea plants in Assam were ignored for a decade.

Meanwhile, the search for ways to get hold of the coveted Chinese plant was on. This was not easy, because in order to maintain their monopoly on tea cultivation, the Chinese had forbidden both tea saplings and tea workers to leave the country – and the latter could face death in case of violation. So of course people tried to smuggle them out, but none of these efforts ended happily. In 1834, Governor-General Lord William Bentinck decided that it was time to make serious efforts to grow tea in India. A tea committee was set up, and its secretary, George James Gordon, was sent to China to collect samples.

In Assam, Charles Bruce made renewed efforts to sell his locally sourced Assamese tea. Realizing that the reason for the inferior quality of the brew was not the plants themselves but the way they were processed, he had spent the previous ten years working out various techniques. For the second time, he sent his tea leaves, differently processed this time, to the experts at the Botanical Gardens, who liked it and declared that it was not very different from the Chinese variety in quality.

Gordon returned from China, bearing a few grudgingly given tea plants. He reported that he was not allowed to be present during the selection and packaging of the plants and suspected they may have been of inferior quality. He did, however, manage to talk to a couple of plantation workers and picked up some secrets of tea processing. The reputation of the Chinese plant was such that, although suspected to be of inferior quality, it eclipsed the discovery of the Assamese plant. Bruce was instructed to plant the Chinese variety in his tea garden in Chubwa alongside the Assamese one.

What followed was disaster. None of the Chinese plants

survived. But before dying, they managed to cross-pollinate the Assamese variety, creating a hybrid that did not survive either. Not one to give up, he set up a new garden in the town of Sadiya and was careful this time to plant only the indigenous Assamese variety.

These survived, and cultivation began. This garden soon grew, and other estates started in Assam, but they were never a great success commercially, although cultivation was steady. Perhaps a deeply entrenched conviction that Assamese tea could never rival Chinese tea, coupled with high labour costs and difficulty in retaining labour, led to the first ever tea company facing bankruptcy in 1843.[ii]

So this brings us to One Tree.

One Tree was the name of the charming little cottage that was Dr Archibald Campbell's home in Darjeeling. (It is now called Beechwood Estate.)

596 — Darjeeling. View from Beechwood.

Figure 1: A view of Darjeeling city from Beechwood Estate during the 1850s.

[ii] The Assam Tea Company was later revived, and by the 1870s did very well for itself.

When Dr Campbell lived here in the 1840s, the view from Beechwood was a little different from what is seen in the picture. The only public building in the entire town was a drab white bungalow with an iron roof – the office of the superintendent. Dotted about this building were some thirty-odd houses. There was no church or bazaar, but a single motorable road wound some 16 miles around the main station. The view of the Kanchenjunga in the backdrop, however, was as magnificent as ever.

During the course of his work, Campbell had made a trip to Kumaon, at the foothills of the Himalayas, where he found tea saplings that had made their way from China (perhaps with Gordon). These he planted in his backyard. To his utter delight, the plants thrived!

Campbell did his homework and followed the methods used by Chinese plantation workers, whose secrets Gordon had managed to unveil. The leaves were therefore plucked at the right stage, with two young leaves and a bud, and withered, rolled, oxidized, dried and sorted in all the correct ways, resulting in a brew of fine black tea – fresh, aromatic and packed with a punch that would signal the end of Chinese monopoly.

Campbell's little backyard soon resembled a miniature tea estate. Camellia sinensis was the variety that he planted, which would go on to become famous as Darjeeling tea, considered the 'champagne of teas'. The year was 1841, and it was confirmed at the little garden of One Tree that Darjeeling was *the* place to grow tea. Darjeeling tea also became India's first GI product (Geographically Indicated), with its quality linked to its geographical location, and therefore not permitted to be cultivated anywhere else in the world. And why not? Because factors such as altitude, rainfall and sunshine all play an important role in determining the taste, and these are often unique to the geography. Dr Campbell grew his plants at an altitude of 2,000 m, and it has since been found that this is the ideal altitude for the very best Darjeeling tea.

We know today that bushes from different gardens within Darjeeling produce teas with different flavours because even a few hundred feet of difference in altitude will subtly alter the flavour. And that is not all; if the soil is too moist or too dry, you will destroy the quality – the moisture has to be just right, as does the amount of sunlight. The ideal gradient for the slopes is between 60 and 70 degrees in order to provide natural drainage during rains. Teas growing in the upper reaches are considered better, as the clouds protect the bushes from too much sunlight. Most importantly, tea buds at this altitude grow very slowly, allowing the flavour to develop.

Darjeeling, with plenty of slopes at differing altitudes, blessed with cool and moist weather, and rainfall averaging 50 to 60 inches a year, was just what the doctor had ordered. All these features combined to give Darjeeling tea its unique flavour, now termed 'Muscatel' and 'Exquisite Banquet', evocative of a distinctive musky spiciness and floral aroma.

The year 1841 was also witness to another happy event: the wedding of Archibald Campbell and Emily Ann Lamb, daughter of Dr John Lamb of the Indian Medical Service. Emily Ann was born in Malda, Bengal. Her mother Juliana hailed from one of the oldest Euro-Indian families, the Crommelins, who had served in India since the 1700s. Dr Lamb also had an extended family in India; his brother George went on to become the head of the Indian Medical Service. Archibald and Emily got married in the picturesque environs of Darjeeling, and together they would go on to have twelve children.

Also multiplying with abandon were the tea saplings. Campbell's neighbour down the road, Johann Andreas Wernicke, a Moravian missionary who had abandoned his mission, had also planted a few saplings. Wernicke's efforts later blossomed into the Tukvar estate, one of the first commercial tea plantations in Darjeeling. Soon, other neighbours began planting tea, experimenting at various altitudes and finding the best places to grow specific varieties. Little gardens grew into small farms, small farms into commercial estates, and then there was no looking back.

A Skirmish with Sikkim

An estate requires a workforce, as does a health resort, and you will recall that Darjeeling was sparsely populated during this time. So Campbell's administration started encouraging Nepali immigrants and also tried to create a workforce out of the indigenous tribes. The latter, with their propensity to be nomadic, did not take to the idea of working in tea gardens, nor were they very impressed with health resorts, but Nepali immigrants were happy to find work. They were particularly helpful when the tea estates started expanding, as the industry was labour intensive. This led to a speeding up of the growth and transformation of a little garden experiment into a commercially viable proposition.

Another factor in the industry quickly catching on was that Campbell generously distributed tea seeds to the now growing number of British settlers, and many succeeded in cultivating the plant. He also introduced a policy of grant of lease of land from the government to those interested in setting up large estates. Trade fairs were organized at the foothills, where growers from neighbouring provinces of Tibet and Nepal could come with their agricultural products and other wares to trade. Prizes were given to high-quality produce, making this a very popular event. Naturally, the economy of the region grew.[4]

Sir Joseph Dalton Hooker, the famous botanist (and a close friend of Sir Charles Darwin's), who visited Darjeeling in 1848 and lived there for three years, was no doubt witness to this transformation. On a mission to collect Himalayan species of flowers for study, he was welcomed by Brian Hodgson, the British Resident, who was also a keen naturalist.

Hooker arrived at a pleasant hillside resort where a few people were engaged in growing tea. Four years later, he departed from a hub of trade, of not just tea but also salt, borax, gold dust, woollen goods and even ponies from the neighbouring provinces. Darjeeling was definitely on its way to becoming the centre of trans-Tibet trade. Hooker was indirectly responsible for the annexation of more territory from Sikkim into Darjeeling, as we shall see presently.

The last few weeks of Hooker's stay proved adventurous for Campbell. Not satisfied with collecting exotic species of flora within the Darjeeling area, Hooker wanted to study Sikkim's flora as well. An application earlier made to the raja by the governor-general on behalf of Hooker had been rejected, as the raja was not particularly friendly with the British at this time. Recall that Darjeeling used to be under his dominion not too long ago. Having seen the rapid growth of Darjeeling, he regretted gifting the territory to the British, and by refusing permission for an Englishman to enter his country, he was showing his dissatisfaction with the earlier deal.

Campbell, however, sent a separate message to the raja, informing him of his plans to accompany the botanist into Sikkim. When Campbell and Hooker entered Sikkim, they were refused entry to the raja's durbar. This was not much of a loss to Hooker, who had made detailed and thorough notes on the indigenous flora in the region, but for a superintendent to be refused admittance, in open breach of protocol, was cause for worry.

However, Campbell retained immense goodwill among the people of Sikkim, especially among the oldest and most respected families. They more than compensated for the raja's snub, extending a warm welcome to the visitors, plying them with food and drink and gifts of silk and lace. Campbell and Hooker had thoughtfully brought with them pretty chintz dresses for the daughters of their host. Soon, many other families came to greet them, but none from among the raja's relatives nor his dewan's (who was the real power behind the throne, and, Campbell suspected, the reason behind the hostilities).

They were utterly unprepared for what happened next. On their way down the mountains out of Sikkim, they were accosted by a large troop of sepoys armed with knives and spears. They assaulted Campbell, rained blows on him and knocked him down. Then they bound his hands and feet and moved him to a tent. Campbell's coolies were also bound. Hooker they were unsure what to do with and simply held him immobile without using excessive violence.

For several days, Campbell and Hooker were imprisoned in separate tents and allowed no contact with each other. Through the kindness of one of the Tibetan guards, Hooker was relieved to learn that no grievous harm had come to Campbell, other than bruises on the head and a black eye, but the treatment meted out to him was far from civil.

The dewan's men who had carried out this attack were continuing to rough up Campbell, demanding a new treaty for the province of Darjeeling. This they hoped to extort by twisting the cords that bound his hands with the use of a bamboo wrench. Campbell retained his presence of mind and told them that whatever assurances he may give under pain would certainly not be followed up by the governor-general's office.

After a month of holding them in captivity in vain, the dewan switched to conciliatory tactics, which, in Hooker's words, resulted in their being 'less disagreeably watched'.[5] Meanwhile, word had reached Darjeeling of the imprisonment, as also a letter from Hooker to the governor-general despatched through a friendly Lepcha sepoy. The British immediately sent troops to the Sikkim border, after which Campbell and Hooker were released without bloodshed. It didn't end so well for the raja, however, as his lease of Rs 6,000 was withdrawn and a portion of his kingdom annexed to make British displeasure clear.

Campbell, as Superintendent of Darjeeling, was given civil charge of the newly annexed provinces as well, but, as one unnamed author of an anthropological journal paper notes, 'without any addition to his pay or allowances'.[6] This was in spite of Campbell's request for an increase in allowance to compensate for the increased labour (something that had also been recommended by a special commission) and the new province being estimated to fetch an additional income of Rs 40,000 to the government.[7]

Could it be because of Campbell's bold march into Sikkim? Did this one act displease someone in high authority so much that all his other efforts were disregarded? So much so that a detailed claim for additional pay, not just for himself but also to carry out administrative tasks, should have been ignored?

DARJEELING'S REMARKABLE POPULATION GROWTH

By 1852, the population of Darjeeling had grown to over 10,000 – a hundred times the number at the time of British acquisition – and this included the permanent residents (whose homes numbered seventy), army personnel in the newly commissioned barracks for the Hill Corps regiment, and Nepali immigrants who came in droves to work in the tea gardens.

A fully functioning sanatorium had been constructed, a bazaar built, and yes, a jail as well. Campbell was careful to model the justice system in alignment with tribal beliefs and systems, while taking progressive steps such as the abolition of forced labour. The number of tea gardens also grew, encouraging more migration from other parts of India.

This rapid surge in population had the effect of somewhat diminishing Darjeeling's reputation as a 'disease-free' zone. And one of the first affected was Dr Campbell himself. While touring the lowlands one day in 1852, he contracted a severe fever from which he never fully recovered. A second attack four years later left him weaker still, and he was advised to go to England on sick leave. This he did – after twenty-nine years of continuous service in India.

On his return in 1857, while elsewhere in India the predominant sight may have been one of turbulence, in Darjeeling, Campbell was greeted with a pretty sight. The tea seedling that he had planted in 1841 had spread beautifully, covering, some said, a circumference of 50 feet.[8] In less than a decade, the number of tea gardens would grow to thirty-nine, yielding 21,000 kg of tea a year.[9] (Today, eighty-seven tea estates spread across roughly 19,000 hectares produce 10 million kg of tea per year).[10]

Now that an industry was established, Campbell concentrated on the logistics of connectivity. He took an active part in promoting the construction of a road from Calcutta to Darjeeling and was later consulted on the development of the best route for a railway line between the two places. In keeping with his vision of making Darjeeling a self-supporting settlement, he encouraged cotton and silk cultivation in the Terai region and held extensive correspondence with the Manchester Cotton Supply Association to ensure a market.

Dr Campbell retired in February 1862, by which time he had served for thirty-five years without any increase in pay or allowances,[11] or even a basic recognition of his role in transforming the economy of Darjeeling or his anthropological studies documenting tribal culture and arts. We know of his works only through the large number of papers he published in various journals, and we must be particularly indebted to Dr Hooker for meticulously recording his travels in the Himalayas, from which we can piece together much of Campbell's work.

We also have information from government reports of that period, recorded by special commissioner Welby Jackson. In a report made in 1853, a decade after Campbell was given civil charge of the region, the special commissioner observed in his very first sentence that 'whatever has been done here has been done by

Dr Campbell alone'.[12] Following this, Jackson enumerated several developmental measures taken to transform the 'inaccessible tract of forest', including cultivation of tea, coffee and European fruits, abolition of forced labour, opening up of the market – all resulting in a revenue of Rs 50,000 within the first few years. Jackson made it a point to note that Campbell was particularly sensitive to the culture of the local tribes, and the justice system and other developmental measures did not infringe upon their way of life but instead empowered them economically.

'It is to the personal character of the superintendent that this success is due,' wrote the special commissioner, 'and to the admirable temper, deliberation and forethought with which he has acted throughout; and this success would have been greater had he received more support and more ample means of carrying out the sound views which he entertains … If actual work and the importance of it be considered, there is no comparison between the mere political duty of a Resident, and the toil and tact required in performing the task assigned to the Superintendent of Darjeeling.'[13] Heartening words, but they did not help Campbell much.

Money was certainly not a motivation for Campbell. There was a drive stronger than that in the indefatigable doctor. For, post-retirement, while residing in London, he devoted all his energies to bringing the produce of the Himalayas to the British public. He exhibited Darjeeling teas at international trade fairs and was also the director of a Darjeeling tea company for a short while. He was an active member of the Anthropological Institute, the Royal Asiatic Society, the Ethnological Society, and the Indian section of the Society of Arts.[14]

He died in 1874, aged sixty-nine, and is buried in the churchyard at Upton-cum-Chalvey.[iii] An obituary published in the

---

[iii] Curiously, Upton-cum-Chalvey contains the grave of another hill station founder, John Sullivan (1788-1855), who established Ooty or Ootacamund

Journal of the Society of Arts highlights his stellar achievements and comments: 'His efforts were prompted by no hope of honour or reward, for be it said, to the shame of our administrators, that neither then, nor at any [time after], was any honorary distinction or post of emolument at home bestowed upon him.'

WHAT PRICE OUR PRIDE?

While the high status that Darjeeling tea enjoys the world over invokes a great sense of pride in every Indian, the industry is not without criticism. Environmentalists have decried forest lands being turned into tea estates and have not been kind to Campbell's policy of encouraging migration into Darjeeling as this shook up the indigenous tribes and took away the pristine quality of the hills.[15] As the hill sanatorium turned into a popular tourism destination, it brought with it all the usual ecological problems in spite of having large forested areas declared 'protected'. The development debate is an eternal one, and it helps to look at all sides of the picture. Economic development and ecology almost always need a judicial trade-off. It is not as if our own cultivators and administrators have maintained a better balance.

While it may be disturbing to know that today the forest cover around Darjeeling has reduced to a mere 38 per cent[16] of the total land area from being nearly all forest 150 years ago, we must not lose sight of the fact that after two decades of tea cultivation by Campbell, by the mid-1850s, the forest cover around Darjeeling accounted for nearly 87 per cent. So it would be hardly fair to blame Campbell for how we may have managed our forest resources. After all, Shimla, which grows no tea, has a mere 36 per cent forest cover today.

In any case, the understanding of the ecological implications

---

in the Nilgiris in south India. (Thanks to David Davies for pointing this out.)

of commercial crops is a matter of hindsight, where everyone has a 20-by-20 vision. In his time, over two centuries ago, Campbell's actions were dictated by nothing but goodwill towards the region, and not by motives of personal enrichment.

There is, however, no denying the fact that India's economy and pride have both gained significantly from Darjeeling's tea. For 150 years, livelihoods in the hills have been sustained by the tea industry and its associated businesses such as packaging. The industry accounted for 10 per cent of the total labour force employed in the country in 2002, with a majority of the workers being women. Forty per cent of the produce is exported, making India the world's largest exporter of tea.

While stressing that sustainable cultivation practices are key and protection of forests paramount, the authors, never happier than when sipping a cup of the best Darjeeling chai, leave you with a refreshing bit of trivia to enjoy with your steaming cup. Sir Joseph Dalton Hooker, known to name species of flowers after the friends he made during his travels, immortalized Dr and Mrs Campbell by giving their names to two varieties of the beautiful rhododendron – rhododendron campbelliae and rhododendron campbellii.[17] He also named the majestic Himalayan deciduous tree with pretty pink flowers magnolia campbellii in honour of Dr Campbell. Hooker took this species back home, where it changed the face of British gardens forever,[18] just as tea did the valleys of Darjeeling.

7

Getting India on Track

R.M. Stephenson and John Chapman:
The Men Who Shrunk India

R.M. Stephenson
1808–1892

John Chapman
1801–1834

ROWLAND MACDONALD STEPHENSON'S DREAM WAS, to say the least, audacious. The year was 1841, and the Industrial Revolution was at its pinnacle in Europe. There had been great innovations in locomotive engineering; England, France, Germany and Austria were criss-crossed with railway lines, and wherever the railways went prosperity followed. One man, however, thought beyond the boundaries of his continent. His dream was 'to girdle the world with an iron chain, to connect Europe and Asia from their furthest extremities by one colossal railway'.[1]

He wrote of extending the European railway line (then

completed till Belgrade) to Constantinople, from where it would enter Tehran, and chug on to Herat, Kandahar, and finally Sibi (in present-day Pakistan), from where it was just one hop by steamer to Bombay, and onward by train again to Calcutta.[2] This would reduce the travel time from England to India from three months to just ten days. There was just one catch – there was no railway line in India[i] and no one knew how to go about laying one.

As most big ideas go, Stephenson's too was dismissed with just two words – 'Wild idea!'

STEPHENSON'S EARLY DAYS

This man with the wild ideas was born in London on 9 June 1808 to Rowland Stephenson, a banker, art collector and politician. Stephenson senior was highly respected and did very well for himself, except for one bad investment decision, which unfortunately was enough to trigger the complete collapse of his bank, following which he disappeared and was later found living in self-imposed exile in America. This apart, the family was quite distinguished, being from the long-established Cumberland family, with an ancestor, Edward Stephenson, briefly serving as governor of Fort William (Bengal Presidency) in 1728.

Unfortunately, details on the life of Rowland Macdonald Stephenson are rather sketchy in the public domain, and we are constrained to weave as much cloth as we can from the few strands of information that have been available to us.

---

[i] There was in fact one short experimental track in Madras, built in 1835, but the carriages were drawn by human or animal power to transport building material, and it therefore does not officially qualify as India's first 'real' railway. This later became the Red Hill Railroad.

From the Harrow School Register, we know that Stephenson was there between 1823 and '24 (see fourth name in figure). Exactly where he graduated from remains veiled in the fogs of time, but there is evidence that after completing his formal education, he joined his father's bank. But this was a very brief career as the bank bankrupted in 1828, following his father's unwise investment. Fortunately, he managed to land a job at one of the biggest engineering firms of the day, Gospel Oak Ironworks.

Since he had no previous engineering training, he was taken as an agent at their London office. However, the engineering side of the business soon caught his interest and he began to spend all his spare time in learning mathematics and engineering principles. He went further, frequently travelling from his London office to the factory, observing the workers and the manufacturing processes, and lending a hand when permitted, thus rounding off his learning with a few practical lessons.

In 1838, he became the secretary of an association called The Comprehensive Company for Establishing Regular Steam Communication with India. While being involved with this, he realized how efficient long-distance travel resulted in progress and prosperity for all parties involved, and gave rise to new business to boot. Specifically, he saw how improved steam travel had brought India and England closer in terms of trade and culture, and he could not help thinking, against the backdrop of great railway engineering works carried out in England, of the huge impact a land route between the imperial power and the promising colony would have. This was when he had his audacious idea of connecting London and Calcutta by rail.

Well, we know that this colossal railway line never materialized, but the last leg of the project certainly did – the railway line within India – and here is how it happened.

Not Such a Wild Idea, After All

Stephenson sensed that the mood in England was not right for grand ideas just then. This was because all the frenzy around the railway industry had resulted in multitudes of railway companies breaking out like a rash all over the country. Many of these were incompetent but had attracted huge investments simply on account of being in the railway business, and had failed to deliver. Following a series of losses, investors were wary and tended to view grand plans with suspicion. Stephenson, therefore, decided to move to uncharted territory.

In 1843, he moved to Calcutta along with his family, and one big dream.

Calcutta was then the most happening city of the British colonies. From its base here, the East India Company controlled not just its interests in India but all of South-East Asia, including Penang and Singapore. It was a hub of international trade, with players ranging from private ship owners, bankers, merchants and agents to the landlords of Calcutta. One of the cogs in this machinery was a prosperous coal mine in Ranigunj, from where coal was loaded onto boats and sent to Calcutta via the Damodar river for export. The mine was owned by an acquaintance of Stephenson's, a merchant prince called Dwarkanath Tagore.[ii] When Stephenson visited this coal mine, he was astonished by the scale of problems with river transport. The dangerously varying levels of the Damodar made it unpredictable, and losses were inevitable when the river flooded. This place was just crying out for a railway.

It was to Tagore that Stephenson first proposed the idea of laying a railway track between Ranigunj and Calcutta, and extending it all the way to Delhi via Benares. Tagore responded

---

[ii] Dwarkanath Tagore was the grandfather of Rabindranath Tagore and one of the first Indian industrialists and entrepreneurs.

with enthusiasm, and even offered to raise one-third of the capital for the portion of the line running between Ranigunj and Mirzapur (near Benares). He had previously worked with Stephenson to promote a river steamboat company under his Anglo-Indian managing agency, Carr, Tagore and Co.[3] The partnership had been fraught with strife, and this was perhaps why, as you will see, they did not eventually collaborate, although their views regarding the laying of the railway line were in alignment.

Having secured some level of support from the merchants involved, Stephenson turned to the government for support. The East India Company's enthusiasm was lukewarm. They were doubtful of the feasibility of laying tracks on unknown ground, and even if that were done somehow, they were not confident that the investment would bear commensurate returns with just goods transport, as they believed that the 'natives' would never prefer this new mode of transport.

Stephenson bided his time. While letting the government work out its priorities, he started putting his ideas down in writing. A paper called the *Englishman* (then owned by Tagore, and later by Stephenson) published Stephenson's well-articulated arguments for the immediate need for six railway lines in India connecting Calcutta, Delhi, Bombay, Hyderabad, Madras, Bangalore, Calicut, Arcot, Trichy (Tiruchirappalli) and Tinnevelly (Tirunelveli).

For a year he wrote, stressing two main advantages – one for the military to help move its troops quickly, and the other being the obvious economic benefits of connecting ports with the interior regions for transport of raw material.

The government began to warm up to this idea, finally.

THE BIRTH OF THE EAST INDIA RAILWAY

In 1845, Stephenson went back to England and started a company called the East Indian Railway (EIR). Dwarkanath Tagore did not join him, but instead established a rival company called the Great Western Bengal Railway Company. However, Tagore died the following year, sadly without witnessing the revolution that the railways were to bring. Stephenson meanwhile began to promote his company in earnest by publishing pamphlets outlining his idea and garnering popular support.

In 1847, he returned to Calcutta along with two assistants and conducted a thorough survey of the proposed route from Calcutta to Delhi via Mirzapur. Having gone over every inch of the proposed route himself, he presented a report with detailed statistical information that strongly pressed for investment in the venture while cautioning that expenses would naturally be subject to some uncertainty. Being the shrewd businessman that he was, he proposed that if the government would grant the land free of cost, the railways would become profitable even without considering any increase in passenger traffic.

This was perhaps the clincher in making the government view his proposal with more favour, for while it was indisputably held that the railways in India would benefit the company, the volatile monetary situation in London and political changes in India made the preliminary negotiations circumspect. After lengthy discussions, a contract was drawn up between the government and the East Indian Railway Company, in which financial terms and areas of control were detailed.

The government insisted on appointing independent surveyors to verify Stephenson's data. Some of them submitted reports stating that the cost of maintenance, operations and depreciation would be much larger than the estimated revenues, if any, leaving no surplus. Others opined that the 'natives' would be disinclined to travel by rail, preferring river transport instead, when speed was not an issue (as it was bound to be cheaper). There were even some who stated that weeds and other native vegetation would 'choke up the lines'.[4]

Stephenson was indefatigable in his pursuit of the project, as documented in a resolution of the shareholders of the East Indian Railway Company recorded in 1849-50: 'That in consideration of the services rendered by Mr R. Macdonald Stephenson to this Company, and of the extraordinary exertions made, and the risks encountered by him, in introducing the railroad system into India, embracing three journeys to India and the survey of many hundred miles of railroad – it is the feeling of this meeting that he should be allowed a compensation for himself, and his family after his decease, by way of a percentage on the net profits which, over and above 5 per cent, shall be received by the shareholders on the capital invested in the experimental section of railway now contemplated, and that the Directors be requested to take into consideration the rate of such percentage and submit the same to a future meeting of the proprietors.'[5]

In 1850, Stephenson, along with resident engineer-in-chief George Turnbull,[iii] finalized the design of the first section of the railway line from Howrah to Pandua, with a branch line to the Ranigunj collieries.

ANOTHER MAN, ANOTHER STORY

Meanwhile, on the western coast of India, another Englishman had a similar dream. If Stephenson's impetus was movement of coal, this man was driven by cotton and its transportation from central India to the ports.

His name was John Chapman and he had just become promoter of a joint-stock company called the Great Indian Peninsula Railway, with a vision to construct a network of railway lines

---

[iii] George Turnbull stayed on in India, overseeing all the major railway constructions, up until the Benares line in 1863. He is often acclaimed as the first railway engineer of India.

starting from Bombay, with one branch heading north-east, and the other branch winding its way down south. The year was 1845.

Born in Loughborough, Leicestershire, on 20 January 1801 to the town's clockmaker, John Chapman was a man of many talents. Educated at a small school run by a Reverend, he displayed an extraordinary skill with mechanical gadgetry at an early age, no doubt inherited from his father. He was also a keen linguist and taught himself Greek and French. Growing up, he developed (what was for that time) radical political views that he did not hesitate to voice, particularly his abhorrence to slavery. Additionally, he became the secretary of a peace society and taught at Sunday school.

In 1822, he set up his first business venture with his brother – a factory to manufacture machinery required for the bobbin-trade (colloquially called the 'insides' of machines). The factory did good business, and he was able to expand and set up his own steam engine to run it.

In 1824, Chapman married Mary, daughter of John Wallis, who owned a lace factory in Loughborough. He became involved in the running of both factories. For the next few years, he witnessed much prosperity but not for long. In 1836, Europe was hit by economic depression. Within no time, Chapman found himself staring at bankruptcy, all his assets gone, his business in a shambles, and his finances in ruins. But he was made of tough stuff. Picking himself up, much like Stephenson did after his father's bank's ruin, Chapman moved to London to try and put his skills to use.

In London, Chapman found work as assistant to mathematical instrument makers and supplemented his income by teaching mathematics in his spare time. London, during this time, was witness to great strides in mechanical engineering. The famous horse-drawn Hansom cab had just hit the streets, and its inventor Joseph Hansom was in the process of filing for a patent. Chapman's keen eye, however, spotted areas of improvement, particularly with regard to the safety of the driver. He also introduced smaller wheels for easy manoeuvrability and designed doors that opened on the side rather than the back. The last was the most popular modification as it prevented people from leaving the cab without paying. In due course, Chapman received a patent, and the modern design of the cab was built upon his modifications, but the name Hansom remained. Another noteworthy mechanical feat of his was the design of a 'flying machine' called Ariel. It never flew, but sixty years later, the Wright brothers' machine that took off from Kitty Hawk in North Carolina in the US had many similar design elements.

Chapman also wrote extensively on topics ranging from politics to engineering. One of the magazines he wrote for, the *Mechanical Times*, devoted the bulk of its pages to the most happening industry of that time – the railways. Chapman's interest and knowledge of the railways grew. So did the ideas.

Sensing a saturation of growth in England, he looked eastwards to make a foray into the railway industry and came to India in 1845.

He faced the same initial reactions to his idea of a railway line in India as Stephenson had – scepticism, dismissal and even ridicule. And like Stephenson, he too was dogged, persevering, gifted with pen and tongue (but perhaps on the brusque side), and managed to gather enough support to form a company. However, the similarity ends here, as things did not go very well for him, with investors in England pulling out of railway companies in droves. One of the companies to suffer was the GIPR, whose stock plummeted by 50 per cent in 1847. For the second time, Chapman lost everything he had.

Any reasonable man might have given up at this stage, but as we have seen consistently, outstanding results are seldom achieved by reasonable men. Chapman persevered.

During the next few months, he lived in near penury, but this only made him work harder. He continued to focus his pitch on the financial benefits of regular supply of raw cotton made possible by an effective railway network. He never presented the railways as an end in itself; to him, it was always a way of optimizing the cost of the logistics of moving cotton. This went well with the commercial establishments he rallied. To the parliamentarians, he spoke of strengthening security in the event of a rebellion (which in fact did happen a decade later).

Chapman was clearly a master marketer. His perseverance, along with the economic turnaround in the following year, helped push the Court of Directors at the East India Company towards backing the idea. Contracts were negotiated between the government and the GIPR, as well as with R.M. Stephenson's East India Railway Company. In March 1849, the contracts were formalized.

The contracts were in the nature of a quasi-public-private partnership arrangement, where ownership, control and risk would be shared between private companies (such as GIPR and EIR) and public entities (like the East India Company), anchored and secured by public guarantees. The ninety-nine-year operating contracts were structured such that the private companies would carry the construction costs of the new railway network while owning the relevant operational arms. In return, the East India Company (the public partner) would guarantee the railway shareholders a 5 per cent return on their capital investment, along with free use of land. The deal was sealed.

This would sound like the victory bugle, but for Chapman, sadly, it was not. Often, when dealing with the bureaucracy, it is not so much about what is said as about how it is said. After all, mediocrity often thrives on form rather than substance. Chapman had always been a very direct man. He did not go out of his way to please those in authority, as is evident from his scathing criticism of the functioning of the East India Company: 'One of the most notorious modern examples of the incompetency of a government as a trader is that of the East India Company after it became a government,' he wrote in his book *Principles of Indian Reform: Being Brief Hints, Together with a Plan for the Improvement of the Constituency of the East India Company, and for the Promotion of Indian Public.*

He went on to elaborate in the following comment, which interestingly could well pertain to any of our recent governments: 'Amongst the most remarkable instances of failure of this kind [in the public works domain] are those of the old Governments of India. They almost never made a road, in our sense of the word road; and when they did make one it was for the convenience of the Government, not of the people. They left ruins behind them at their successive seats of power almost all over the country, amongst which, by the way, are very few ruins of bridges; and they never reared a spirit of either enterprise or cooperation amongst the people sufficient, without the Government, even to keep up the works when made.'[6] No, he did not go out of his way to ingratiate himself with anyone.

Over the years, the members of the board of the GIPR had been criticizing his lack of diplomacy, judgment and discretion, although they had no cause for complaint with his work. In 1846, the chairman of the GIPR company, Lord Wharncliffe, had described the railway construction negotiations with the East India Company as 'a task requiring no ordinary share of intelligence, activity, perseverance, integrity and discretion,' and on seeing Chapman's detailed proposal to achieve the same, had commented that his confidence in Chapman had been well justified.[7]

However, after the contract had been successfully signed, the members of the board came out openly against him, chastising him for his abrupt ways and refusing to be flexible. To make matters worse, they offered him a meagre salary and a lowly position as if to taunt him. He believed that he deserved better, especially now that the company was prosperous. The board did not hear him out. He made his displeasure clear and rejected the offer, coating it with colourful words.

Hostility from the board only deepened, and Lord Wharncliffe also made a U-turn. He opined that Chapman's claims were 'untenable, his views unsound, and his terms utterly inadmissible by the Board having regard to the interests of the company'.[8] In 1849, his services were deemed 'no longer advantageous to the company', and he was dismissed from service. His claim for payment was submitted to the East India Company for arbitration and he was awarded a final payment of Rs 2,500.[9]

The GIPR itself, however, continued to do well and maintained a close rivalry with Stephenson's East India Railway. Newspapers frequently reported their progress in tandem, comparing finances and growth in minute detail. In the final race to be called the first railway in India, it was the GIPR that won.

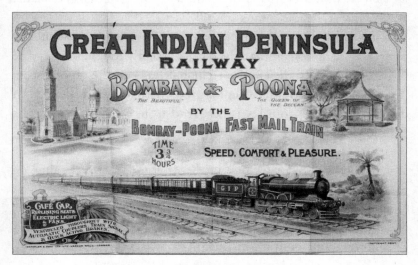

Figure 1: A vintage railway poster.

At 3.35 p.m. on 16 April 1853, amidst thunderous applause, the first passenger train in India[iv] was flagged off from Bombay, accompanied by a twenty-one-gun salute. Its three locomotives – Sindh, Sultan, and Sahib – hauled fourteen carriages with 500 passengers on board. Chugging along the shining new track, the train reached its destination, Thana, in fifty-five minutes, covering a distance of 34 km.

Vast crowds had gathered to witness the spectacle; sadly, Chapman was not among them.

The Press Hails the Inauguration of the Indian Railways

The *Bombay Gazette* dated 18 April 1853 spoke of the inauguration thus: 'Saturday, the 16th of April, 1853, must be a memorable day henceforth forever in the annals of India, memorable as the greatest of battles, and surely more glorious, for peace hath its triumphs as well as war, and this is of them. The Great Indian Peninsula Railway was this day inaugurated!'[10]

The British press concurred, hailing the event which 'would be remembered far longer than the battles recently fought to integrate parts of India into the empire'. The battles, said the report, seem 'tame and commonplace' compared to this achievement.[11] A description of this journey is best read from an extract from the *Bombay Gazette*:

'At half-past three o'clock in the afternoon a royal salute was fired from the ramparts of Fort St George, immediately after which the well-filled train, consisting of fourteen first, second, and third class carriages, drawn by three locomotive engines, and containing in all, it was said, about five

---

[iv] And all of Asia

hundred persons, started from the Terminus at Boree Bunder.

'Tens of thousands of persons surrounded the spot and as the moving mass swept along the way, still there were tens of thousands looking on – men, women, and children – perched on wall tops, on the branches of trees, even in the mast of Arab bughi along the harbour, from windows, and from the tops of temples and of houses, from every eminence around the town; finally, when the train had passed the most densely populated parts, still the surrounding fields were studded with spectators.

'Besides the inhabitants of Bombay Proper, and the neighbouring country, there were in those crowds people from Scinde, from Cabul, from Afghanistan, from Central Asia, from the Persian Gulf, from Arabia, from the East Coast of Africa, and one might say literally from all the ends of the earth. Who shall attempt to describe the emotions which filled and animated those vast throngs of human beings!

'A passenger in the train looking out upon them, as it swept along still faster and faster, could only notice the vivid gestures of some, the silent amazement and awe of others, and the loudly expressed wonder and applause of the greater number. Every Englishman must have congratulated himself on being one of the dominant race that day. The scene was worth to England the addition of many regiments to its army. It has added sensibly to the power of the empire, and will undoubtedly prolong it. It is not merely the inauguration of a railway thirty miles long. It is the commencement of a new era, and while time and history last, the memory of this day can never pass away.'[12]

The Eastern Railway Too Opens

As for the East Indian Railway, they had a decidedly more ambitious project ahead of them compared to the much shorter western line between Bombay and Thana (although even that had involved drilling through a mile and a half of rock in the mountains of the Western Ghats). The British press was continuing to compare the GIPR and the EIR, more so in the wake of the spectacular inauguration, firmly relegating the EIR to second place, declaring that '[the GIPR] keeps itself in advance of the East Indian, both in its operations in the East and the amount of confidence reposed in it at home', according to a news report from the *Railway Times* dated 29 April 1854.[13]

To add to the EIR's woes, they were beset with a series of unfortunate snags right from the time work started. First, a boat carrying a locomotive from England was misdirected to Australia and had to be re-routed, reaching Calcutta only a year later. Another ship carrying carriages met with an accident in the tricky waters of the Hooghly at Diamond Harbour. However, the actual laying of the track was relatively easier than the one in Bombay because of the flat terrain, and work on the first section was completed in September 1854. During the next one year, the 120-mile-long track all the way to the collieries of Ranigunj was complete.

A report in the *English Mail* dated 6 February 1855 said: 'Saturday, the 3rd of February, being the day appointed for the official opening of our rail as far Raneegunge, a distance of one hundred and twenty miles; the vicinity of the terminus at Howrah was at an early hour thronged with an immense concourse of spectators. At the Calcutta side of the river also, the throng was dense, and on very few occasions have the native population displayed greater interest in any spectacle, not immediately connected with the religions they profess, than they did on this occasion.'[14]

As for apprehensions regarding the willingness of the 'natives' to travel on trains, historian G. Huddleston put it best: 'During the eleven months of 1855, in which the line was open from Calcutta to Raneegunge, no fewer than 617,281 passengers were carried, an amount of traffic quite sufficient to satisfy the most sceptical of the travelling propensities of the natives of India, and beyond this there was an immediate development of the goods traffic. Contracts were entered upon to carry over 100,000 tons of coal from Raneegunge to Calcutta, and a quantity of ordinary merchandise was transported, which, though comparatively small, gave hope for the future.'[15]

Figure 2: 'Orion', an early EIR locomotive built in 1859-60.

And Then There Was No Stopping ...

It is said that the first million is the hardest to make. By the same token, once Stephenson and Chapman had opened the field through their pioneer railway companies in India, the landscape was laid wide open for a host of other railways to make their forays. Soon, tracks were being laid in other parts of the country. The Madras Railway Company, over the next few years, laid a track from Madras to Arcot, and this soon expanded to touch the western coast. Similar progress was made in Punjab and central India. But nothing was as challenging as the track through the Western

Ghats. Engineers trained by the famed Stephensons, the father and son duo of George and Robert, pioneering railway engineers (no relations of R.M. Stephenson), were commissioned from London to design complicated tunnels and embankments.

Although European engineers had some experience with mountains, having constructed railroads in the Alps, the ghats were a different proposition altogether. Rocky terrain, steep cliff faces with no footholds, blistering heat, and narrow hairpin bends to navigate – as one would expect, accidents were common. The construction of this stretch took a sad toll. Many workers fell to their deaths into deep ravines from ropes suspended over cliffs. Others simply dropped from the exhaustion of working in the heat.

The central areas of India posed another threat – thick jungles alongside which tracks were being laid exposed the workers to attacks from wild animals, and hundreds are believed to have perished to leopards. However, it was disease that took the highest toll. Dysentery, malaria, typhoid, cholera, small pox and so on routinely broke out in the unhygienic conditions of the construction camps. A startling statistic puts this toll at an estimated 25,000 deaths over an eight-year period[16] – numbers usually seen only during wars or other calamities.

This is even more chilling when you consider an official document that historian Anthony Burton has excerpted in his book *On the Rails: Two Centuries of Railways*: 'The fine season of eight months is favourable for Indian Railway operations, but on the other hand, fatal epidemics, such as cholera and fever, often break out and the labourers are generally of such feeble constitution, and so badly provided with shelter and clothing, that they speedily succumb to these diseases and the benefits of fine weather, are, thereby, temporarily lost.' Burton goes on to comment that 'the notion that lives – and the inconvenient loss of working time – could be saved by providing proper shelter and working conditions does not seem to have been considered.'

Figure 3: Tigers on track.

Casualties occurred among the British as well. Tropical diseases claimed many lives; those who did manage to return to their homeland died soon after, their bodies bereft of strength.

James J. Berkely, the chief engineer of the GIPR and a student of Robert Stephenson, was responsible for designing a major portion of the tracks navigating the Western Ghats. His ingenuity in negotiating steep inclines stands the test of time, as the same design was later used in the construction of railways across the Andes mountain ranges in South America. The stretch that Berkely designed took eight years to build, having twenty-five tunnels, eight viaducts, and approximately 54 million cubic feet of rock to cut through.[17] Unfortunately, he did not live to see the opening of this stretch as he died from failing health when he went to England on a visit.

R.M. Stephenson's health too took a turn for the worse, and he was compelled in 1856 to return to England, where he joined the board of directors of the East Indian Railway Company. In the same year, the government recommended his name to the queen for a knighthood, which was bestowed upon him.

Sir Stephenson lived to the ripe old age of eighty-eight. In 1895, he passed away at his residence in Tunbridge Wells. He remains best known for his work in realizing the dream of constructing the railways in India, as is evident by a mention in his obituary on the difficulties he went through to achieve the same:

'With feeble health, and no knowledge of any native language, he sat for years rarely stirring out of his office, driving with the energy of five men the vast concern. There were difficulties with the Government, difficulties with the native landlords, difficulties with the contractors, and, twice at least, any other man would have retired dead beat; but Macdonald Stephenson never lost heart or patience or temper with any obstacle ... However great the difficulties, he demanded that the work should go on, that nobody should talk of impossibilities, that non-existent labour should be imported, and that the indispensable class of minor contractors, who did not exist and could not be imported, should be created out of the ground; and so the road rolled on till it reached Delhi.'[18]

SOME PERSPECTIVE

Consider this. In 2015, India had a total of about 65,000 km of railway track. When the British quit India in 1947, they left us with 49,300 km, or nearly 75 per cent of the length of railways tracks we have today. In other words, since Independence, we have added tracks at the rate of 0.40 per cent per annum, or about 201 km per annum, or roughly 0.56 km per day.

Or consider this. Even though the city of Jammu had an old railway station built in 1897 with services to Sialkot, Wazirabad and Narowal, the services were terminated in 1947 when India and Pakistan split. Subsequently, a broad gauge railway line between Pathankot and Jammu became available only in 1975. Thereafter, notwithstanding all the sensitivity involving Kashmir and Pakistan, notwithstanding the lack of development of the state of Jammu and Kashmir, notwithstanding the lack of integration of J&K with the rest of India, work on railways to connect Jammu with Kashmir – a distance of 345 km – started as late as 1983, and at the time of writing this chapter (2013), the line is expected to be completed only by 2017! That makes it to an expected rate of 10 km per year or 28 metres of railway line per day.

Compare this with China. China connected Tibet by connecting the final section of the pan-Himalayan Golmud-Lhasa railway (1,956 km) at 5,072 metres above sea level at a surprising speed – 285 km per year. The final section, completed in a record four years, comprised 1,142 km, running across Tibet's snow-covered plateau – dubbed the roof of the world – and presented some unusual difficulties. The engineers had to contend with building on a 550-km frozen belt, with the snow alternately melting and freezing in summer and winter. Workers had to breathe bottled oxygen to cope with the high altitudes but there was not a single death due to this.

Well, it may be that the railways would have entered India eventually in any case, with or without the British. But the pace evidenced by the government of India post-Independence does not inspire a great deal of confidence. The diehard optimists amongst us may yet take heart from the fact that from less than half a mile a year as the national average to about six miles a year (10 km per year) in the case of the Jammu to Kashmir railway, we have come a long way.

And yet, no one may deny that it is definitely an advantage that more than 75 per cent of the job had been done when the British left India, thanks largely to the labours of Stephenson and Chapman. Perhaps only the blindly chauvinistic will hold that the promotional activities of Chapman and Stephenson in the face of scepticism from government authorities and difficult terrain within the country did not hasten the arrival of the railways in India. It goes without saying that many other people contributed to this development, but the efforts of the two gentlemen stand out for their unmatched tenacity in the face of numerous expected and unexpected odds.

Critics have argued that much of the development of railways was to benefit the British empire – to move raw material from the hinterlands to the coasts and so forth. And yet, it must be remembered that neither Stephenson nor Chapman was primarily driven by this motive. They were merely entrepreneurial engineers who were driven by the charm of coal power in one case and optimization of the cost of logistics in the other. The truth is that the duo had to overcome every conceivable opposition from the very British authorities who benefited most from the railways.

One such instance of opposition has been documented by Charles Dickens in his weekly magazine *Household Words*. He wrote of the experiences of an Indian official (whom he does not name) stationed at the Hooghly Board of Revenue. According to Dickens, this is what the official had to say: '... whilst I was in the Muzzypoor district ... some wild speculative interlopers had formed the insane idea of introducing railways into the east, and had bored the [East India] company for all sorts of indulgences and assistance – as though we were not busy enough with our land tax, and our opium monopoly, and our wars. These railway fellows were kept at bay as long as possible, one letter having remained two years unanswered; but at length something had to be done. Assistance was promised in a variety of ways, and official letters were addressed to the several Collectors of districts, directing them to afford every facility and information in their power to those undertakings. I received one of these circulars, and with it a "private and confidential" communication, informing me that I was only to act with the most official formality and to throw every impediment in my power in the way of the railway. Fifteen years have elapsed since the first efforts were made: and last month the first fifteen miles of Indian railway were opened, being at the rate of a mile a year. People in England are amazed at this snail's progress, and set it all down to the natural difficulties of the country: for the ignorant know nothing of the natural difficulties of a 'private and confidential'. A significant and instructive volume might be formed of these confidential communications ...'[19]

While one celebrates the railways as one of the best legacies handed over to us by the British, a lingering suspicion remains that a legacy of another kind – of 'private and confidential' communications instructing officials to throw 'every impediment' in their power – came down to us in its entirety, and is now firmly and unshakably entrenched in our system.

8

A Family Enterprise of Excellence

Alexander Cunningham and Brothers: Prove the Point

Joseph Davey
Cunningham
1812-1851

Alexander
Cunningham
1814-1893

Francis
Cunningham
1820-1875

INDIA IS HOME TO some of the grandest and most ancient monuments in the world. Remarkably, they have withstood the test of time, invasions and general apathy to stand tall today, attracting huge numbers of tourists from within and outside the country. The bulk of our history textbooks are devoted to the study of a detailed chronology of all the empires that ruled this land, some leaving a more indelible mark than the others. We take so much pride in the skill and wisdom of our ancestors, but how do we know what we know?

It is tempting to say that much of Indian history could have been squeezed into an extremely slim volume, but for the efforts Sir Alexander Cunningham – a British army officer and archaeologist. He lived in India during the mid- to late-1800s, a time when little of India's recorded history was available. The Indus Valley was yet to be unearthed, Emperor Ashoka was known only as part of some legend with little historical evidence that he had actually ever lived, and the golden age of the Guptas was yet to be written about. Even a basic chronology of Indian empires was not known.

Who was Alexander Cunningham, and why did he care so much about recording Indian history? Where was he from, and what did he leave behind? Who were his parents, his brothers and sisters, and did they have anything to do with his achievements, or anything to do with India? The answers are fascinating, as a little bit of digging reveals.

The Cunninghams, an ancient Scottish family tracing its lineage back to Norman noblemen of the twelfth century, were at the forefront of numerous clan wars, distinguishing themselves in battle through the centuries before peace finally reigned. A particular branch of the Cunningham family tree settled in the picturesque county of Dumfriesshire, filled with hills, glens, sloping hillocks and lochs – all the right ingredients to inspire poetry. No surprise then that this was home to the poet Robert Burns, whose neighbour James Cunningham was the grandfather of Alexander.

Alexander's father Allan, himself a poet of some note, would often visit Burns and be the first to hear just-composed verses that would go on to become immortal. Later as editor, Allan Cunningham would bring out *The Works of Robert Burns* in eight volumes. Allan also grew close to another great writer of ballads, James Hogg (more famous as the 'Ettrick Shepherd'), and himself composed two original Scottish ballads. This came to the notice of

Sir Walter Scott, another great poet and writer of the time, and a lifelong friendship was forged between them, which would have a bearing on Allan's children's future, along with all the other literary influences that we have mentioned so far.

Allan Cunningham and his wife Jean Walker (formerly a maid in the Cunningham household) had six children – five boys and a girl – all of whom inherited their father's talents with the pen, and carved out distinguished names for themselves. But three of the brothers were not satisfied with just writing. They were keen on pursuing a military career, perhaps heeding to a more distant ancestor's call. It was Sir Walter Scott who used his good offices with the Scottish members of the military to influence the cadetships of the three brothers, and all of them would go on to be most worthy of their father's good connections.

They graduated from the Addiscombe Military Seminary, the East India Company's training academy, with top honours, followed by a professional course in engineering. Of the three, Alexander is best known as the founder of the Archaeological Survey of India, but his brothers Joseph and Francis too deserve space in our chronicle for their significant contributions to Indian heritage, and it is about them that we will read first.

JOSEPH DAVEY CUNNINGHAM – A FRIEND OF THE SIKHS

The story of Joseph Davey Cunningham, the eldest of the Cunningham brothers born in 1812 in Lambeth, London, is rather poignant towards the end. His early life, as it so often happens, was filled with promise. As a student he showed a remarkable aptitude in mathematics, and his father was advised to send him to Cambridge. But young Joseph's heart was set firmly on becoming a soldier, and so he went to the Addiscombe Military Seminary instead. He passed out with numerous accolades (including an expected first prize in mathematics and the sword for good conduct) and proceeded to Chatham, a town to the east of London, to receive training in engineering, before being commissioned into the Corps of Sappers and Miners with the Royal Bengal Engineers.

The fresh graduate arrived in India in 1834, full of enthusiasm and strong letters of recommendation. He was appointed to the Bengal Presidency (one of the most sought-after regions), attached to the staff of chief engineer General Macleod. Three years later, Lord Auckland (then governor-general of India) promoted him to political office. He was appointed assistant to Colonel (afterwards, Sir) Claude Wade, the agent in charge of British relations with Punjab and Afghanistan.

This brought Joseph Cunningham in close contact with the various Sikh chiefs, with whom he developed a deep friendship based on mutual respect and an understanding of culture. This is significant because the Sikhs and the British had always shared an uneasy truce, bordering on the hostile, with the former opposed to any annexation and the latter wary of the temperamental and ferocious chiefs.

In 1838, Joseph was present at the landmark meeting between Maharaja Ranjit Singh and Lord Auckland, which paved the way for a tripartite treaty between the Sikhs, the British and the Afghans (represented by their king Shah Shuja), leading to relatively peaceful conditions in the region for the next seven years. In 1839, Joseph accompanied Shah Shuja's son Shahzadah Timur and Colonel Wade to Kabul, which made him part of the first British advance into the Khyber Pass. In 1840, he was placed in administrative charge of the district of Ludhiana, and the following year was given magisterial charge of the Ferozepur district.

Lord Auckland's tenure as governor-general came to an end in 1842, and with it also ended the delicate harmony he had managed to build. He was succeeded by Lord Ellenborough, who was widely criticized when he conquered and annexed the province of Sindh, a move seen even by many English commentators as unnecessarily belligerent, and which turned the Sikhs against the British. In 1844, Lord Hardinge stepped as the new governor-general into a smouldering pot of discontent that led to a full-fledged war between the Sikhs and the British, termed as the First Anglo-Sikh War.

In all this time, Joseph had become closely acquainted with the Sikh people, their customs and way of life, having lived among them for so long. He began to delve deeper into their history and was fascinated by what he learnt – not least by the fact that no written record of this history existed. It was fortunate that as a reward for his services, he had just been appointed to the political agency of Bhopal in central India.

This was very different from life on the frontiers, especially during the war, and he found plenty of time to organize his considerable knowledge of Sikh history. On his father's advice, he embarked on the ambitious project of writing a book on this subject. He wrote it from the perspective of a historian rather than a British officer, and the result was the comprehensive work, *A History of the Sikhs*, published in 1849, which is even today regarded as a definitive text on the subject.

He wrote with admiration of the honour and bravery of the Sikhs, and in particular of the great Sikh chief, Ranjit Singh. He concluded the book with a heart-breaking account of the Battle of Sobraon (First Anglo-Sikh War, 1845-46), where he described the unflinching valour and indomitable courage of the Sikhs in the face of overwhelmingly superior British weaponry and certain death. But ultimately we learn that the Sikhs were defeated not by these known enemies but the traitors Tej Singh and Lal Singh, the commander of the army and Ranjit Singh's Vizier respectively, who had been bribed by the British to flee the scene of battle, leaving their armies to be crushed. The author does not mince words while summarizing the war, declaring, 'Under such circumstances of discreet policy and shameless treason was the battle of Sobraon fought.'[1]

As soon as this book was published, it was received extremely well by the press as well as scholars. As the first work to document the history of the Sikhs, it was considered invaluable, and the author's authentic research that stemmed from his close contact with the Sikhs was acknowledged. However, the political office of Lord Hardinge took exception to the mention of the treacherous agreement between the British and Tej Singh and Lal Singh. Joseph, who had been present during the negotiations, stuck to his guns, insisting that he had only documented the truth. Also, the fact that Tej Singh and Lal Singh received rich rewards after the war certainly lent credence to his position.

Unfortunately, the book caught the attention of Lord Dalhousie, the new governor-general of India, who was known for his despotic style of functioning. The candour and honesty with which Joseph had described the battle of Sobraon irked him. Swiftly and mercilessly, he rendered the publication of this book a crime. As punishment, Joseph was dismissed from his employment in the political department and sent back to regimental duty. He was shocked by this high-handed oppression of honest recording of truth. As an upright officer and true historian, his prime intention had been to present facts as they had happened, for the benefit of posterity, and not to score short-term political points.

But Dalhousie thought differently. Colonel G.B. Malleson, a later historian, would comment thus on Dalhousie's thoughts, action and their effect on Joseph: 'That an officer holding a high political office should write a book which, by the facts disclosed in it, reflected, however indirectly, on his [Dalhousie's] policy, was not to be endured. With one stroke of the pen, then, he removed Cunningham from his appointment at Bhopal. Cunningham, stunned by the blow, entirely unexpected, died of a broken heart!'[2]

Before his death, Joseph had planned to launch a second edition with some explanations. His preface to the second edition contained this gentle admonition, 'The glory to England is indeed great of her Eastern Dominion, and she may justly feel proud of the increasing excellence of her sway over subject nations; but this general expression of the sense and desire of the English people does not show that every proceeding of her delegates is necessarily fitting and farseeing.'[3]

Unfortunately, he died in 1851, two years before its publication. The book saw numerous editions, became highly respected for its fearless writing and historical accuracy, and is, even today, considered the definitive work on the history of the Sikhs. In the words of Malleson, 'Lord Dalhousie could crush Cunningham, but he could not crush his work. The truths given to the world by this conscientious and faithful historian will forever be the basis upon which a history of the Sikh war, worthy of the name of history, will be written.'[4,i]

Francis Cunningham – A Friend of Mysore

Francis Cunningham, born in 1820, was the youngest of the Cunningham brothers. Like his brothers Joseph and Alexander, he attended the Addiscombe Military Seminary before being commissioned into the Madras Native Infantry. Not much is documented about his military career, save for a note of distinction he earned as field engineer at the defence of Jallalabad during the first Afghan War. In 1850, he was posted to the Mysore Commission where he served as deputy to the chief commissioner, Sir Mark Cubbon (after whom the famed Cubbon Park of Bangalore is named).

---

[i] In 1963, a century after Cunningham's *History of the Sikhs* caused so much consternation among the British officials, another book on the same subject, *A History of the Sikhs: 1469-1839* (Delhi: Oxford University Press, 1963 and 2004) made waves for its comprehensive and thorough research – authored by prominent Indian novelist and journalist, the late Khushwant Singh.

Documentation of his work during service is sparse, but it is known that he contributed to the development of the horticultural gardens at Lalbagh, designed Sir Cubbon's bungalow at Nandi Hills, and possibly a few more quaint bungalows in and around Bangalore. He was also known as a good writer, his talents no doubt inherited from his father.

He retired in 1861 but stayed on in India in the service of the maharaja of Mysore, and it was during this time that he put his writing skills to good use as he lobbied eloquently for the restoration of Mysore to the Wodeyars, who, after having signed a treaty with the British, had maintained sovereignty of their province. This is a story that needs some telling.

Between 1831 and 1868, the British had taken over the administration of Mysore based on the claim (put forth by the then Madras government) that the maharaja had failed to pay the subsidiary tribute as per the treaty of 1799. This treaty had been signed by the Mysore maharaja following the fall of Tipu Sultan, agreeing to pay a tribute to the British which would guarantee his sovereignty. While the maharaja maintained that he had been paying this tribute without fail, the Madras government alleged otherwise, and Lord William Bentinck despatched an intimation to the maharaja of Mysore, 'couched in terms of the greatest severity',[5] that the British government would take over the administration of Mysore.

On returning to England, Lord Bentinck realized that the claims of the Madras government were false and expressed anguish over this deposition. He is known to have repeatedly declared that the supersession of the maharaja of Mysore was the only incident in his Indian administration that he looked back upon with sorrow. This is documented in the *Mysore Gazetter* (Vol. 2): 'He [Lord Bentinck] put it on record that what he had done had been carried out under a grievous misconception of facts, and that he had been misled into action by the "exaggerated representations" of the

Madras government of the time. In his Despatch to the Court of Directors, he could not help expressing "certain doubts both as to the legality and the justice, according to the strict interpretation, of the course that had been pursued".'[6]

Lord Bentinck's successor, Sir Charles Metcalfe, too expressed a similar opinion, terming the maharaja's supersession a 'harsh and unprovoked'[7] measure.

However, the Court of Directors expressed unwillingness to suddenly cancel an existing order. Also, the fact that the maharaja did not have a male heir prompted a few to reason that after his demise the kingdom would naturally fall under British governance. In 1864, therefore, the maharaja made known his intention to adopt a son as his heir and successor. But the supreme government informed him that while he was within his rights to adopt a son as his successor so far as his private property was concerned, no authority to adopt a successor to the State had been given to him.

Francis Cunningham spent his retirement years writing persuasively on behalf of the maharaja. Many of these letters made their way to Lewin Bentham Bowring, the then commissioner of Mysore, urging him to correct the wrong done to Mysore. Though Francis's powerful writing caused him much headache, Bowring wrote this little note on him: 'He wielded a ready and incisive pen, his official letters showing great command of language, in which was often a vein of irony and humour that was unpalatable to the recipients. He had left the Commission before I joined, but had taken service with the Raja at Mysore, his principal duty being to compose the despatches which His Highness sent to the Government about his claims, a task which his literary qualifications enabled him to perform exceedingly well, although his presence at the capital and the encouragement given by him to intriguing parties were a source of some embarrassment to me ...'[8]

The British press, too, took up the cause of the maharaja. The *Daily News* in its issue of 2 August 1866 remarked, 'India cannot be really tranquil so long as the Native Princes entertain the slightest suspicion that the all-powerful British Government is disposed to avail itself of any plausible pretext for annexation.'⁹ A host of other newspapers along with prominent officers and respected public figures strongly opined that this was an opportunity to set an example of British fair play by restoring the throne to the maharaja.

Finally in 1867, Francis Cunningham and all others who had raised their voice in support of the maharaja heard a highly satisfying verdict from the British House of Commons, which voted to restore the Mysore kingdom to the maharaja and recognize his adopted son as his successor. Finally, Francis returned home to continue his literary pursuits, the most notable of which was editing the works of Kit Marlowe in 1870, and those of Philip Massinger and Ben Jonson in 1872. He died on 3 December 1872. Unfortunately, he did not live to see the formal transfer of power to the Wodeyars, which happened only in 1881, nine years after his demise.

Francis stayed in Bangalore till 1870, touching the city in many little ways, most of them undocumented, and the city honoured him by having one of its most multicultural streets named after him – the Cunningham Road.

Alexander Cunningham – A Friend of India

Best known of the Cunningham brothers, Alexander was born in Westminster, London, in 1814, and received his early schooling at Christ's Hospital, which is unique as British public schools go, because it was envisioned as a shelter for the poor and destitute by King Edward III in 1552. After school, it was the good old Addiscombe Military Seminary for Alexander, and then the Royal Engineers Estate in Chatham. He graduated at nineteen and was commissioned into the Bengal Engineers regiment in 1833, following which he spent close to five decades working in India.

Just a few months after arriving in India, he met James Prinsep, whom you ought to be familiar with by now if you have been reading the chapters in sequence. Cunningham shared his passion for philology and archaeology and happily volunteered to assist him in his studies. They studied coins, seals and other artefacts unearthed during excavations, and their research enabled a historically accurate understanding of various Indian dynasties. Their most important contribution, however, was their study of ancient inscriptions found on rock faces and pillars, especially those on the stupas of Sarnath.

Prinsep was successful in deciphering the entire Brahmi script, revealing a whole new body of knowledge to the world. Alexander alongside made detailed drawings of the monuments and carvings. Prinsep had been working on a plan to publish a comprehensive collection of ancient Indian epigraphy, but it was only in 1877, thirty-seven years after his death, that Alexander was able to carry out his wish. *Corpus Inscriptionum Indicarum* was the result, volume one of which contains the first ever description of the edicts of Ashoka.

How It All Started

In 1848, Alexander put in a proposal for the constitution of a formal Archaeological Survey of India. He was turned down. As consolation, however, a small grant was approved for the protection of ancient monuments, based on recommendations from the Royal Asiatic Society. Alexander continued to study archaeology as a serious hobby while serving as an engineer in the army. During this time, he grew interested in the works of Chinese monks Fa-Hian (or Faxien) and Hsuan Tsang (or Xuanzang), who had visited India during the fourth and seventh centuries respectively. They were Buddhist monks, on a pilgrimage to the holy shrines of Sarnath, Sanchi, Taxila, Peshawar, Mathura and Bodh Gaya, among others.

Their works had become available through French translations in the 1850s, a time when the philosophy of Buddhism was gaining prominence among European scholars.

However, there was also the widely held belief that the Europeans were the ones who brought civilization to India, since so little was known of the richness of our history. The discovery of ancient writings and monuments helped the emergence of the contrary view that the India that the Europeans colonized had been preceded by a golden age, and there was much yet to be learnt about her past. A lot of digging had to be done. And Alexander Cunningham decided that he was the man who would do it.

He was partial to Buddhist sites. In 1851, he visited Sanchi, one of the holiest of the Buddhist sites, although this was not known at that time. Local wisdom held that the domes were monuments to a long forgotten king. A young officer, Lieutenant Frederick Charles Maisey, had been employed by the Government of India to prepare drawings of archaeologically important monuments in central India. Alexander joined him and conducted extensive excavations at the site. Many buildings were crumbling, their carvings broken or defaced, but from what was visible, it was evident that they were valuable enough to be preserved.

In the days when scientific methods of excavation were unknown, Alexander and his team did their best to discover without destroying. In order to explore the contents of a stupa, they would sink a shaft from the top of the dome all the way down to the ground level to explore the inside. They found a number of relics, including stone tablets with inscriptions in the Brahmi script. Working closely with James Prinsep, who was fifteen years his senior, Alexander concluded that the inscriptions were of Buddhist nature, dating back to Emperor Ashoka's time, or even earlier. Maisey prepared some beautiful drawings of the monuments, capturing each detail of ancient workmanship accurately and artistically.

View of the Great SANGCH TOPE, from E.N.E.

Figure 1: Plate VII from Cunningham's *The Bhilsa Topes*, a two-page spread of a beautifully hand-drawn view of the Great Sanchi Tope.

Soon after, Alexander and Maisey visited Bhilsa, now known as Vidisha, located near Bhopal. Their meticulous study of the carvings and inscriptions led to the book *The Bhilsa Topes*, published in 1854. This work is regarded as the first attempt to understand Buddhist history through its architectural remains. In the preface, the author modestly describes his work thus: 'The discoveries made by Lieutenant Maisey and myself, amongst the numerous Buddhist monuments that still exist around Bhilsa, in Central India, are described – imperfectly, I fear – by myself in the present work.'[10]

At that time, there was no evidence available for establishing the chronology of medieval Indian dynasties and very little of our history was accurately known. Our puranas and literature were liberally sprinkled with myth, and even if the facts were drawn out, there was no way to reliably date them. The Sri Lankan Buddhist epic Mahavamsha spoke about Emperor Ashoka, but no physical evidence had been found yet.

Alexander Cunningham began that process when he painstakingly excavated and made sense of the glorious ruins at Vidisha and Sanchi. He says in the book, 'In illustration of the ancient history of India, the bas-reliefs and inscriptions of the Bhilsa Topes are almost equal in importance to the more splendid discoveries made by the enterprising and energetic Layard in the mounds of the Euphrates. In the inscriptions found in the Sanchi and Sonari Topes we have the most complete and convincing proof of the authenticity of the history of Asoka, as related in the Mahawanso.'[11]

RETIREMENT AND AFTER

Alexander retired from service in 1861, but that was just the beginning of another glorious career. He put forth a fresh proposal for the constitution of a formal Archaeological Survey. Lord Canning, the viceroy at the time, accepted the pitch. Alexander was appointed the first director of the Archaeological Survey of India, and the scope of this department was limited to 'an accurate description – illustrated by plans, measurements, drawings or photographs and by copies of inscriptions of such remains as deserve notice, with the history of them so far as it may be traceable, and a record of the traditions that are retained regarding them'.[12]

He planned a detailed survey of north India, taking a cue from Hsuan Tsang's itinerary. Just five years later, however, the Archaeological Survey suffered a setback because the then secretary of state, Sir Stafford Northcote, had a different view on the policy towards heritage sites. He advised the new viceroy, Lord Lawrence, to decentralize and entrust the local governments with identifying ancient monuments in their jurisdiction. The ASI was disbanded and instead four independent units in Bombay, Madras, Bengal and the Northwestern Provinces were constituted. They were entrusted mainly with studying different architectural styles and documenting them. And so, protection, conservation and fresh excavations took a back seat.

In any case, the Archaeological Survey was never conceived as a permanent department. It was expected that all of India's monuments would be documented within a few years, and onus of preservation would be on the local governments, and there would be no reason for a central department to exist. However, a liberal wave of thought sweeping across Europe at that time held that imperial powers had a responsibility towards preserving ancient sites in their colonies. Lord Lawrence had a change of heart and reinstated the Archaeological Survey in 1871, with Alexander as director-general. He was entrusted with 'a complete search over the whole country, and a systematic record and description of all architectural and other remains that are either remarkable for their antiquity, or their beauty or their historical interest.'[13]

However, historian John Cumming notes, 'the Director-General lacked the help of a proper staff of provincial surveyors, so that virtually he "directed" no activities but his own, and those of the assistants working under him. With what ability and industry, however, General Cunningham performed his task is abundantly evident in his twenty-three volumes of Reports descriptive of twenty-three years' touring.'[14]

Alexander clearly went beyond the call of duty in personally touring all the places in the survey plan. The result of all his research and travel was the publication of *The Ancient Geography of India*, which he based on the travel records of the Chinese pilgrims Hsuan Tsang, Fa Hien and Sun Yong, as well as his own extensive travels across north India. He writes in the preface, 'My own travels also have been very extensive throughout the length and breadth of northern India, from Peshawar and Multan near the Indus, to Eangoon and Prome on the Irawadi, and from Kashmir and Ladak to the mouth of the Indus and the banks of the Narbada. Of southern India I have seen nothing, and of western India I have seen only Bombay, with the celebrated caves of Elephanta and Kanhari.

'But during a long service of more than thirty years in India, its early history and geography have formed the chief study of my leisure hours; while for the last four years of my residence these subjects were my sole occupation, as I was then employed by the Government of India as Archaeological Surveyor, to examine and report upon the antiquities of the country. The favourable opportunity which I thus enjoyed for studying its geography was used to the best of my ability; and although much still remains to be discovered I am glad to be able to say that my researches were signally successful in fixing the sites of many of the most famous cities of ancient India.'[15]

Perhaps his most important contribution (one of many) is the restoration of the temple at Bodh Gaya, the legendary site of Buddha's enlightenment. When Alexander first visited this area in the state of Bihar, the only visible relic of an ancient empire was buried under centuries of sand. Along with J.D. Beglar[ii] and Rajendralal Mitra,[iii] he painstakingly dug through, careful not to destroy precious artefacts in his quest for knowledge. He uncovered many previous attempts to restore this ancient temple, some of them haphazard, and used his engineering skills to restore the main temple. Several generations of archaeologists continued the restoration, and today this can be seen as the Mahabodhi temple

---

[ii] J.D. Belgar was an archaeologist at the ASI, mostly known for his work in restoring dilapidated temples in the Manbhum region (present day Purulia district of West Bengal).

[iii] The first Indologist of Indian Origin, Rajendralal Mitra was appointed librarian of the Asiatic Society in 1846. He was a keen historian, philologist and an important figure in the Bengal Renaissance. He became the first Indian president of the Asiatic Society in 1885.

complex, a UNESCO World Heritage site, 'one of the earliest Buddhist temples built entirely in brick, still standing in India, from Gupta period'.[16]

Many ancient cities including Rajgriha, Sankisa, Sravasti and Kausambi were identified by Alexander's excavation efforts. Ashoka's monolithic capitals, relics of the Gupta era and post-Gupta era, and numerous Buddhist stupas came to light and have now made their way into our history textbooks and tourist brochures. The monastery at Sarnath, where the Buddha first preached dharma to his five disciples is a prime example. Innumerable inscriptions were deciphered, leading to a documentation of Indian history that left no doubt as to the magnificence of her past.

It is evident that Alexander regarded the Buddhist phase of Indian history as her richest and concentrated on excavating these sites. This is perhaps why, in 1872, having visited Harappa, the site of one of the oldest civilizations in the world, and having picked up from there a seal out of interest (which was possibly the most ancient artefact ever to be found in India or anywhere in the world at that time), he did not attach too much archaeological significance to the site save for the description that it was 'the most extensive of all the old sites along the banks of the Ravi'.[17] Perhaps the historical importance was not immediately evident as the site had been robbed of bricks (possibly for use in building the local houses). He did, however, publish the Harappan seal, but it was only half a century later that any serious interest began to develop to excavate and study these sites.

Alexander retired again in 1885 after having surveyed most of north India, published twenty-three volumes of ASI reports on ancient monuments and authored five books. And at seventy-one, he was not done yet. He had a third career ahead of him, as a numismatist. He moved back to England and devoted all his time to the study of coins, of which he had built a formidable collection over the years. He authored another book during this period, which is widely regarded as the definitive work on Indo-Greek coins, titled *Coins of Ancient India* (1891). He also published papers in the *Numismatic Chronicle* and the *Journal of the Asiatic Society*. A major part of his coin collection is now housed in the British Museum.

He was deservedly knighted in 1887. This was a fitting tribute to Sir Alexander Cunningham – the man whose work laid the foundation for documenting most of medieval Indian history, and who expended immense personal time and effort in restoring the ancient monuments to the glory that we now take so much pride in.

9

Demystifying Malaria

Ronald Ross's Hunt of the Anopheles Mosquito

1857–1932

WHY WOULD ANYONE SPEND a lifetime peering into the innards of mosquitoes, repeatedly subject himself to hundreds upon hundreds of mosquito bites at the grave risk of contracting the biggest scourge ever to afflict mankind, with death as the most plausible reward, especially when one had far more comfortable options available as the son of an English general?

Most would not. But most people are not made of the same DNA as Ronald Ross, who did all of the above and thus came to hold a particularly special place in India, which has easily been the biggest beneficiary of his work – identifying the female Anopheles mosquito as the carrier of malaria and devising effective anti-malarial measures. His work would painstakingly unfold after he came to India as a young army officer, more or less forced to do so by his domineering father. His single-minded dedication to unravelling the mystery of the mosquito would come to save millions upon millions of lives in Asia, Africa and elsewhere.

And that is why today, there are roads and institutions named after him. Kolkata has named the road connecting Presidency General Hospital to Kidderpore Road in his honour – Sir Ronald Ross Sarani. In Hyderabad, the hospital of regional infectious disease is named after him: Sir Ronald Ross Institute of Tropical and Communicable Diseases. The building where he toiled and zeroed in on the Anopheles mosquito is not far from the old Begumpet airport in Secunderabad. The building today is a heritage site, and the road leading up to the building is named Sir Ronald Ross Road, even if the building does not exactly buzz with footfalls. Ludhiana also has a Ross Hostel in the Christian Medical College.

Here was a man who took to medicine against his inclination. He showed himself to be, at best, mediocre at what his father wanted him to study. He was equally mediocre at what he believed actually interested him – namely, arts, an army career, literature, drama and the like. Against his own innate interests, his father, a tough British army officer, continued to push him towards medicine. And yet, because of his sincere work ethics, his power of observation and his ability to connect dots, he went on to win not just the Nobel Prize for medicine but left an indelible mark on the course of medical history.

BORN IN INDIA

Ronald Ross was the son of an army officer serving in India. His father, born in 1824 – in due course to be impressively acclaimed as General Sir Campbell Claye Grant Ross – was himself a son of an army officer, Lieutenant Colonel Hugh Ross. Ronald's mother was Matilda Charlotte Elderton, the daughter of a London-based lawyer. While recorded knowledge of Sir Campbell and Lady Matilda is limited, we do know that they tied the knot in 1856.

At the time, Campbell Ross was a young officer posted in Almora, the beautiful hill town nestled in the lower reaches of the Himalayas, sitting atop a horseshoe-shaped ridge in central Kumaon, in present-day Uttarakhand, protectively flanked by rivers Kosi and Suyal. The British occupied Almora in 1815, wresting it away from the Gurkhas. Nineteenth-century Almora was a breathtakingly beautiful hill town that was home to a huge diversity of flora and fauna.

It was in the lap of this picturesque town that Ronald Ross was born – on 13 May 1857, the year of India's first war of independence. He would be the first of nine more siblings to come – a respectable-sized Ross family indeed.

Figure 1: Leper Asylum, Almora, around the 1880s.

Early Life

India in general and the peripatetic life of a soldier in particular did not afford the best of education for the first son of an ambitious army officer. So Little Ronald, not yet ten, was sent home in

1867 to study in the British seaside town of Ryde, where his early
education was shaped in two small schools. From here, a couple of
years later, in 1869, he was sent to a boarding school at Springhill
in Southampton, the largest city in the county of Hampshire, on
the southern coast of England.

In this commercial city, where he spent the next five years,
Ronald excelled in mathematics and received a book as a prize,
the book being an introduction to astronomy – *Orbs of Heaven*
– which in due course would ignite some of his interest in
mathematics. Ronald did seem to possess some unusual talents.
At sixteen, while at Oxford and Cambridge, he took up drawing
as an optional subject and came out on top in the examinations.
He made a pencil copy of a Raphael painting, 'Torchbearer', in
no time. Perhaps motivated by this, he thought his calling was in
the arts.

In the following year, however, he announced a change of
plans; he would rather be a writer. In his final year at Springhill,
he penned forgettable verse. His first epic was the story of Edgar
– a dreamy ineffectual character. At seventeen, he was perhaps at
the age where ambition shifts like mercury. He even wondered if
he shouldn't enter a naval or army career, like his father. But of
course his ambitious father would have none of that nonsense.
Like most parents in our own country today, the old man told
him in very precise terms what he expected of the young Ross in
terms of a serious career.

Later in life, Ronald would muse, 'I wished to be an artist, but
my father was opposed to this. I wished also to enter the army or
navy; but my father had set his heart upon my joining the medical
profession and, finally, the Indian Medical Service, which was then
well paid and possessed many good appointments; and, as I was
a dreamy boy not too well inclined towards uninteresting mental
exertion, I resigned myself to this scheme.'[1]

Clearly, young Ronald respected and trusted his father enough to give up his own ambitions. Ergo, in 1875, Ronald Ross ended up at St Bartholomew's Hospital, also known simply as Barts, in Smithfield in London to study medicine. Barts was the oldest hospital in the whole of Europe, established in 1123 and then re-founded by King Henry VII in 1546. The hospital occupies its original grounds even today. It was also the same hospital where Sir William Harvey had conducted his researches on the circulatory system in the seventeenth century.

Not unlike a number of average youngsters in today's eminent institutions, Ronald spent a lot more time composing music and writing poems and plays than on his medical studies. It was also about this time that Barts received a woman patient from the marshes of Essex, complaining of a severe headache, fever and muscular pain, with bouts of feeling extremely hot and extremely cold. While Ronald quite correctly diagnosed the case as that of malaria, he was rather surprised that he should find the tropical disease in an Essex resident. His unusually detailed examination frightened the poor lady away for good and left Ronald unable to prove the prevalence of malaria right there in England.

This episode seems pivotal in the life of Ronald Ross in some ways. A reluctant medical student until then, something in the profession seems to have evoked in him a keen interest in mosquitoes. So much so that even as a student nearing the final year of his studies in 1878, he worked on a thesis to prove that a parasite that caused a disease in humans could also infect a mosquito.

His interests may have been varied and his academic performance average at best, but it was increasingly becoming evident that he had a sharp and inquisitive mind. What with his preoccupation with his extra-curricular interests, he passed his Member of the Royal College of Surgeons examination with mere three days of preparation and a friend helping him. But it was without notable distinction. He also simultaneously took the

Licentiate of the Society of Apothecaries (LSA) examination at his father's bidding – and failed.

Brigadier General Campbell Claye Grant Ross, who was keen to see his son well settled in India, preferably in the Indian Military Services, before he superannuated, was unabashedly disappointed.

Happy to idle away his time though Ronald was, his father was not one to suffer idlers. A threat to cut his spending allowance sent him scurrying aboard a ship commuting the London-New York route as the vessel's surgeon. To keep his father happy, he made another attempt at the LSA in 1880, managing to scrape through in the lowest quartile, just as his father was decorated as a Knight Commander, Order of the Bath (KCB).

Ronald was appointed a surgeon in the Indian Medical Services in April 1881 and sent for a prescribed course in military medicine, before he set sail for India on 22 September. He landed at Bombay on 23 October to join the Indian Medical Services in the army the following year – twelve years after he had first left for England.

Upon arrival in India, Ronald, thanks to his rather mediocre performance in the LSA examination, was at first relegated to the Madras Services, considered the least attractive of the three presidencies – Bengal, Bombay and Madras. Then he was posted as acting medical charge to the 17th Madras Infantry for six months at Vizianagaram in present-day Andhra Pradesh. Later Ronald would reminisce about his life in Vizianagaram as being 'better than the home life of a professional man in England'.

Soon he was attached to the Presidency General Hospital in Calcutta, where his early work on mosquitoes would take shape. Visitors to Kolkata can still find the beautiful red brick Hospital a stone's throw from the Victoria Memorial. Today, it houses the Post Graduate Medical Education and Research Centre. The hospital, built in 1707, was probably the first hospital ever built in Calcutta and was initially meant specifically for the British army. It was probably only after 1770 that it was thrown open to non-Europeans. A plaque outside the institute informs you: 'In the small laboratory 70 years [ago] to the southeast of this gate surgeon Major Ronald Ross IMS in 1898 discovered the manner in which malaria is conveyed by mosquitoes.'

RONALD'S MEDICAL CAREER IN INDIA UNFOLDS

As late as the turn of the nineteenth century, in the British Army in India which at the time had a strength of about 180,000 men, some 75,000 were found to be suffering from malaria and admitted into various hospitals. Later in the century, in 1897 alone, an estimated 5 million Indians would succumb to malaria. As late as 1935, 1 million Indians probably died of malaria.[2]

From the ancient times, it was assumed or hypothesized that malaria spread through bad air; hence the name mal-aria – Latin for 'bad air'. It was only in the mid-nineteenth century that a race among scientists for uncovering the truth about malaria took off earnestly. So working in India amidst thousands of soldiers frequently coming down with malaria, a keen observer of patients like Ronald Ross could not have remained out of this race for long.

Following his transfer to the Presidency General Hospital, Ronald spent the next seven years in Calcutta, though from here he was constantly shunted to various other places, including Bangalore, Burma and the Andaman islands. His experience in Madras and Calcutta undoubtedly brought him close to the strange battlefields in which thousands of soldiers suffered and died every day at the hands of an enemy called malaria. Ronald from here on revealed an inquisitive and dogged mind which he would bring to bear on solving the mysteries of malaria.

Some kind of association of mosquitoes with certain diseases was not entirely unknown. For instance, only five years before, around 1878, one Patrick Manson had discovered that mosquitoes could be hosting the parasites responsible for filaria. On another tack, around 1880, another scientist, Charles Laveran, had shown that the malaria parasite must in all probability spend some part of its life cycle outside the human body.

Since both mosquitoes and malaria seemed to be abundant where bad air prevailed, mosquitoes were beginning to emerge as serious suspects in relation to malaria, and if, as Laveran had shown, malaria probably had a carrier, the mosquito was the proverbial butler – the prime suspect in murder mysteries – and the mosquito-malaria hypothesis was born.

In 1883, Ronald Ross built a small residence at Mahanad village on the Bandel-Burdwan line in West Bengal and set up a little laboratory there. He would frequent this house every now and then, journeying from Calcutta on his mosquito-collecting forays to scout Mahanad and nearby villages, rich in mosquitoes, and peer into the innards of the pests for hours in his makeshift lab, trying to establish whether they could be responsible for malaria in some way.

His work was interrupted when he was transferred to Bangalore as acting garrison surgeon. Here he was attached to the well-known St John's Hospital. For most, the transfer would have been excuse enough to let the study they had commenced to be disrupted. But not for Ronald Ross, who seems to have found a mission in life – to solve the puzzle that mal air, mosquito and malaria together seemed to present.

In Bangalore, Ronald, still only in his twenties, found his living quarters quite acceptable, though he could hardly relax here, what with the buzz of mosquitoes forever assaulting the eardrums everywhere in his house. He noticed too that his own quarters seemed to be a much more preferred destination of rendezvous for these mosquitoes than the adjoining ones. The specific beacon to which the mosquitoes were drawn in swarms seemed to be an old drum with some stagnant water near one of the windows. A closer inspection of the contents of the barrel revealed a mass of tiny grubs writhing in the water. Clearing the water seemed to reduce the attraction of the barrel to the mosquitoes.

A very basic demonstration of cause-effect relationship between stagnant water and mosquitoes seems to have revealed itself to Ronald. It appeared reasonably clear to him that the stagnant waters were the very lifeline of mosquitoes and if the lifeline could be cut, namely, all stagnant pools of water removed, that should remove the mosquitoes as well. And if mosquitoes were at all responsible for malaria, cleaning up the stagnant pools should help; if not, at least one would be rid of the buzzing pests. But it would appear that Ronald did have a strong intuition about the role of mosquitoes in carrying malaria – intuition that is often the first building block of inventions and discoveries.

Greatly enthused by his find (which the Romans had figured out thousands of years ago, even if Ronald did not know it), he did what most enthusiastic youngsters do. He took his idea to the adjutant of the unit he was attached to, suggesting that all stagnant pools of water in the entire unit and the officer's mess be dried up post-haste to make the area free of the mosquito menace. The adjutant did what most adjutants do. He took obvious pride in his men being deployed for more useful purposes and refused to have them do such menial tasks as clearing up garden tubs, coffee mugs, tea cups or flower vases and so forth strewn around the mess.

In 1885, Ronald was seconded for a while to the Anglo-Burma war. The next year, he also spent some time in the Andaman islands and was left with little time to pursue his interests in mosquitoes. Even though these secondments disrupted his enquiries into the social lives of mosquitoes, he wasn't quite wasting his time. Even if he was unable to pursue bacteriology, he wasn't going to give up his study of mosquitoes altogether. He reared mosquito larvae as one would rear goldfish in one's spare time and distinguished two main varieties (grey – Culex, and brindled – Stegomyia).

He also used his time sharpening his mathematical skills, which would one day stand him in good stead in analysing his medical research results. He wrote poetry, developed his musical skills and penned mediocre plays and novels (even publishing them at his personal expense). But like a slow burning fire, his interest in tropical diseases, particularly malaria, continued. At the time malaria was estimated to be killing between 5 and 10 million people in India every year. Moved by this large-scale devastation caused by malaria, Ronald penned this verse:

In this, O Nature, yield I pray to me.
I pace and pace, and think and think, and take
The fever'd hands, and note down all I see,
That some dim distant light may haply break.

The painful faces ask, can we not cure?
We answer, No, not yet; we seek the laws.
O God, reveal thro' all this thing obscure
The unseen, small, but million-murdering cause.[3]

By 1888, he sensed that he wasn't heading anywhere, either with his medical or his literary pursuits, and decided to take a furlough to England. His efforts at replicating Laveran's findings weren't successful. He realized too that his literary skills weren't much – what with his having to publish his own works and the only readers being his friends and family. His father had been perspicuous indeed.

He decided to join the Liverpool School of Tropical Medicine to get himself a diploma in public health, taking newly offered courses on bacteriology, figuring that if he was to live and serve in tropical India, he might as well add to his understanding of tropical diseases and medicines.

It was also at this time that he found his wife, Rosa Bessie Bloxam, daughter of Alfred Bradley Bloxam, a merchant in

Southampton. They were married in 1889. In due course, the couple had two daughters, Dorothy and Sylvia, and two sons, Ronald and Charles.

RESEARCHES IN MALARIA

We made a brief reference to Laveran and Manson earlier. Well, the last quarter of the nineteenth century was also the period when these two leading scientists were getting set on the starting line of the race to decode the malarial puzzle – namely, exactly what caused malaria and how it spread. The first off the block seemed to have been Charles Louis Alphonse Laveran (1845-1922), a French physician, who, while working in Algeria in the 1880s, had taken a blood smear from a patient who had just died of malaria, and after observing the parasites in the smear, identified the protozoa (single-celled parasite) responsible for malaria. Technically, he was the first to observe the exflagellation[i] of the malarial protozoan – an observation that would ultimately lead to the unravelling of the malaria puzzle.

Laveran had named the protozoan Haemamoeba malariae. He found that the protozoan appeared in different forms in humans, especially in liver and brain capillaries. He was the first to propose that the malaria parasite must in all probability grow outside the human body, and not inside. This implied that the parasite must be transported into the human body by an external carrier or a vector. This conjecture came to be known as the vector hypothesis. This was a significant step in the understanding of malaria.

Patrick Manson (1844-1922), a parasitologist from Aberdeen, Scotland, was the next of the aforementioned duo on the malarial

---

[i] Long, thin, swiftly waving tapering outgrowth of cells of several microorganisms such as protozoa, used as a means of locomotion.

trail, who in due course came to be regarded as the father of the very branch of tropical medicine. Graduating in medicine, he worked long years in Formosa (Taiwan) and China in the local missionary hospitals. It was here that he first noticed filarial worms in the lymph vessels and microfilariae in the blood of patients infected with filariasis or elephantiasis (the condition that gives one exaggeratedly swollen legs, resembling an elephant's, and hence the name).

He used the data to work out the life cycle of filariasis. His observations showed that most victims of filariasis came from areas that were thickly infested with mosquitoes. With his painstaking efforts, in 1878, he discovered that the filarial worms were present in the human blood samples only during the night and were absent during the day. He conducted many of his experiments on his gardener, who was infected with filariasis. He would let mosquitoes feed on the poor patient's blood as he slept and would later collect and dissect the mosquitoes under a microscope.

He discovered that the filaria thrived on 'the digestive juices' of the mosquito, while it developed only as far as the embryo stage in the human body. Thus he hypothesized that the mosquito must have a role in the life cycle of the filarial parasite and hence the spread of the disease. In due course, this would give rise to his mosquito-malaria hypothesis.

By destiny, it was left to Ronald Ross, who had had his own brief familiarity with the mosquito as a student at Barts, to pursue the suspect, lose it, find it again and finally after laborious exertions prove the mosquito-malaria hypothesis.

Ronald's Return to India

Having married during his furlough in 1889, he returned to India with his wife, armed with his new diploma and a resolve to tackle malaria all out for the next few years. He arrived in Madras city and was posted once again to Bangalore, attached to a small military hospital. Of Bangalore, he would say, 'In spite of its beautiful climate, Bangalore was not a very healthy place and did not suit me; my studies on malaria did not advance, and I began to be oppressed again with some of the moods of 1888.'[4] He formally renewed his investigations into malaria in 1892.

About the same time, Manson was following up on his earlier work on filaria with a shift of focus to malaria, and would publish his own results, leading to the mosquito-malaria hypothesis in his paper 'On the Nature and Significance of the Crescentic and Flagellated Bodies in Malarial Blood', which was published in the *British Medical Journal* on 9 December 1894. In this paper, he observed that it wasn't unlikely that each form of malarial plasmodia involved a particular species of mosquito as a carrier. This was great intuition, as it would turn out. Manson's work seemed to further underscore the earlier findings of the early '80s by Laveran.

So returning to his malarial research, Ronald tried to take off where he had left his earlier investigations. He remembered his earlier failures in replicating Laveran's results on his own. Eager to independently reconfirm Laveran's findings, Ross soon acquired notoriety at the military hospital where he was posted, for his keen quest of malarial patients and his propensity to puncture their fingers for blood, so that he could peer at the blood smears under the microscope, trying to locate the malarial protozoans.

On Manson's advice, he captured mosquitoes and fed them on malarial patients by releasing them into their mosquito nets and then tried dissecting the mosquitoes – only to find nothing. Apparently the mosquitoes weren't biting. Figuring that may be the mosquitoes were too subdued to bite, he tried hand-rearing mosquito larvae in captivity and tried releasing them on the hapless patients. Months of hard work and another round of dissections later, there was still nothing.

It was the summer of 1895. He was despondent. He turned to Patrick Manson for guidance, which the great scientist willingly offered not only just then but throughout their lives. Ronald took to writing to his newfound mentor virtually every other day, updating him on his findings. Manson advised him to let mosquitoes bite malaria patients and then allow those mosquitoes to lay eggs and hatch out grubs in a bottle and then give that mosquito water to healthy individuals to drink to see if they contracted malaria.

Not one to give up, Ronald managed to find a volunteer in one of his local assistants, Lutchman, and a few other brave-hearts, for the promise of a suitable compensation, to actually have the unpalatable drink of water in which mosquitoes had died. To his delight, Lutchman developed a high fever shortly. The high soon turned to low when Lutchman recovered within a week and walked away with his compensation.

Down and out on morale and exhausted, Ross turned to writing verses again. But Manson frantically tried to buck up his spirits, writing, 'Above everything, don't give it up. Look upon it as a Holy Grail and yourself as Galahad and never give up the search, for be assured that you are on the right track. The malaria germ does not go into the mosquito for nothing, for fun, or for the confusion of the pathologist. It has no notion of a practical joke. It is there for a purpose and that purpose, depend upon it, is its own interests – germs are selfish brutes.'[5]

It may be that Manson was also concerned that someone else may beat Ronald to the final line, leaving him (Ronald) no credit for all his hard work. So he counselled in one of his numerous letters: 'The Frenchies and Italians will pooh-pooh it, then adopt it, and then claim it as their own. See if they don't. But push on with it and don't let them forestall you.'[6]

But much as he tried, Ronald was unable to detect the crescent-shaped protozoans that Laveran had found. His conviction that

Laveran must be wrong or even that his data could be fudged only grew stronger.

Unfortunately for him, he was unaware that the protozoal parasites of malaria are much smaller than those of filariae and so much more difficult to locate within the human body. Neither he nor his peers who shared his scepticism of Laveran's findings were aware that their failure was largely due to the under-developed microscopic techniques of the times. Nor had it helped that the illustrations in Laveran's articles had been of rather poor quality. Besides, Ronald was not being institutionally supported in his malarial researches. He was carrying out much of his malarial work in his own time and at his own expense and could not have afforded a better microscope even if it had existed. So little wonder that he had been unable to spot the protozoans in the human bodies.

Thus frustrated, for a time he toyed with the hypothesis that malaria was caused by some sort of bowel poisoning, and had nothing to do with Laveran's finding. So he started working on this hypothesis and even went on to publish his bowel-related malarial conjecture. And yet, he was unable to convince himself about his own conjecture. Something deep down continued to nag him. It was far too much coincidence that bad air and mosquitoes should be so closely related and yet mosquitoes should be entirely innocent of having a role in the spread of malaria.

Inspiration came his way as he read and re-read Manson's original articles on filariasis. His argument had been that if a mosquito could be a vector for filaria, there was no reason why it could also not be a vector for malaria. He came to this conjecture because he argued, and rightly, that if the phenomenon of exflagellation of protozoa observed by Laveran was true, it could be explained only if the malaria parasite originated outside the human body and was nurtured in moist conditions in relatively low temperatures – conditions that hold inside the stomachs of insects.

In his works published in 1894, Manson had already shown that mosquitoes played a crucial role around a particularly sensitive and important phase of parasitic development during which exflagellation occurred inside the stomach of the mosquito, and the free flagellum penetrated through the stomach wall to develop into a larval malaria parasite. Thus he was nearly convinced that malaria could not pass from one human to another without the mosquito being the carrier. The great Manson was not far off the mark, even if he did not find the time to close the loop on his hypothesis and instead exhorted his protégé Ronald to try and do so.

The combined evidence relating to malaria from Laveran and Manson was becoming far too compelling for Ronald to ignore. He wrote again and again to Manson, sharing his results and asking for leads, which the generous Manson more than willingly gave at each stage, so that Ronald could prove his (Manson's) own mosquito-malaria hypothesis and identify the exact vector that incubates and carries the malaria protozoan.

While Ronald worked tirelessly to verify the first part of Manson's theory, namely, that 'the crescent-sphere-flagella metamorphosis was intended to occur in the mosquito's stomach', his real problem was with the second part of the theory, that 'the liberated flagella' live in the insect's tissues, from which they enter drinking water. He was unable to find any evidence in this direction. In fact, this didn't appear to be true at all, no matter how hard he tried to prove it.

Ronald Ross Cranks Up Malarial Research

Ross, prodded on by Manson, continued collecting mosquitoes, hoping to get enough humans to be bitten by these. He figured out that the best way to get the mosquitoes hungry and bite humans was to moisten their beds and the mosquito nets. He even tried to get himself bitten by the mosquitoes – all in vain. Manson advised him to try his experiments with different varieties of mosquitoes. So he assiduously started looking for and collecting a variety of mosquitoes and dissecting them, trying to establish the lifecycle of the malarial parasite inside the viscera of each variety of mosquito. But success continued to elude him.

He was transferred once again, this time to the medical college of Osmania University in Secunderabad. By now, Ronald had started wondering if he had been working with the wrong variety of mosquitoes – the common household variety, which after all may not be the relevant insect, going by Manson's hypothesis. He decided to investigate the species active in the more malaria-infested areas. He had some trouble obtaining leave because his malarial researches were on his personal account, but succeeded and proceeded to the notorious malarial valley of Sigur Ghat on the Mudumali-Kalhutti-Ooty route. He trekked through malaria-infected areas but didn't encounter too many mosquito populations.

This was April 1897. Trekking and cycling for days through the Kalhutti pathways, he finally came down with a bad bout of malaria. It was a time when Manson's conjecture that malaria was contracted by consuming malaria-infested water still dominated his thinking. He racked his memory in vain to recall where he might have consumed mosquito-infected water, but could recall no such incident.

He recovered in a sanatorium in Kunoor and returned to Sigur Ghat to identify the culprit. He had by now more or less convinced himself that the common household mosquitoes (Culex and Stegomyia) could not possibly be the malaria-bearing species, and yet unfortunately these were what his staff was mostly able to capture back in Bangalore.

Returning to Sigur Ghat, scouting all day on foot for mosquito-ridden puddles, he simply could not find a single puddle with mosquitoes in that dry heat. Even in a region which was supposed to be the epicentre of malarial cases, he found quite a few natives who were drinking from the local river or irrigation streams and who had never fallen prey to malaria. He more or less concluded that mosquitoes, notwithstanding the circumstantial evidence, 'could play no essential part in the propagation of malaria'.

Nevertheless, he announced a reward for every mosquito brought to him dead or alive.

For his troubles, he was rewarded with a singular mosquito of a species with dappled wings that he had not encountered before. This was of great significance, as we shall see shortly.

Weak from the bout of malaria and his intense labours at the ghat, he returned to Secunderabad, leaving his family in Bangalore. In the soul-sapping heat, it was nearly a month before he could summon his willpower to put his eyes to the microscope once again.

In later years, he would recall this period of July 1897, in his own prose and verse-ridden words, reconstructed from his notebooks, letters and memories: 'On arrival at Secunderabad, after the severe labour in Ootacamund I felt my first violent reaction against the microscope. And could scarcely bring myself to look through mine for a month.'[7]

It was during an evening spent sitting pensively on one of the boulders found on the outskirts of Hyderabad city that Ronald observed a vulture and a dead jackal in the desolate vicinity. And fate had destined this vision to be his epiphany. For some reason, the sight put a thought in his mind: 'Why not see whether mosquitoes, fed on malaria blood as before, contain any of the mosquito parasites which I had found in the Sigur Ghat?' The thought seems to have inspired Ronald, as he would later recall, 'I do not boast of my premonitions because they seldom come true! But at that time I was certainly much exalted in spirit and said to myself, "One more effort and the thing will be done."'[8]

So the next morning in the summer of July, he pushed himself like an athlete on his last lap. And his efforts are best captured in his own words:

'At first I toiled comfortably, but as failure followed failure, I became exasperated and worked till I could hardly see my way home late in the afternoons. Well do I remember that dark hot little office in the hospital at Begumpett, with the necessary gleam of light coming in from under the eaves of the veranda. I did not allow the punka to be used because it blew about my dissected mosquitoes, which were partly examined without a cover-glass; and the result was that swarms of flies and of "eye-flies" – minute little insects which try to get into one's ears and eyelids – tormented me at their pleasure, while an occasional Stegomyia revenged herself on me for the death of her friends. The screws of my microscope were rusted with sweat from my forehead and hands, and its last remaining eye-piece was cracked!'[9]

On the morning of 15 August 1897, one of his 'mosquito men' (Indian staff hired to help him with his mosquito collections) brought him some larvae in a bottle which were different from the usual Culex and Stegomyia larvae he was familiar with. The very next morning the hospital assistant excitedly drew Ronald's attention to a small mosquito sitting on a wall, with its tail sticking outwards. Ronald placed the mouth of a bottle slowly over it ('if one jabs the bottle quickly, the insect always escapes sideways' – Ronald's tip to any would-be mosquito catcher) and killed it with tobacco smoke. A close inspection of the sundry spots and lines on the wings of the tiny creature convinced him that the pest was of the same dappled wing variety, a single specimen of which he had encountered in Sigur Ghat. And yet when he dissected it, he found nothing unusual.

The same afternoon the worthy hospital assistant returned to inform Ronald that the unfamiliar larvae that had been fetched the previous day had hatched into dapple-winged mosquitoes inside the bottle. Ronald counted about a dozen 'big brown fellows with fine tapered bodies and spotted wings'. These were similar to the dapple-winged creature with its tail sticking outwards he had caught in the morning, but bigger. What could be the significance of the difference? Could these be the females, while the smaller specimen had been a male?

It so happened that Ronald had just come across a malaria patient, one Hussain Khan, whose rain-soaked bed had attracted mosquitoes in droves, causing the poor fellow to come down with malaria. Ronald had talked him into becoming one of his human guinea pigs. He placed the hapless Khan inside a mosquito net and let loose his mob of the dirty dozen dapple-winged mosquitoes inside the net. Once these mosquitoes had feasted on poor Khan's blood overnight, the next day he managed to capture ten of the blood suckers alive, with two dead for the tally. He dissected two of them at once, finding nothing of use.

On the morning of 20 August, which he would later call Mosquito Day, he found three more of the remaining mosquitoes dead, leaving only five alive. He dissected one of the bloated cadavers, with no result. He dissected three more of the remaining ones, drawing a blank – no parasites. Ronald was irritated with his staff for not having found more of the same larvae. By 1 p.m., with his eyes bursting with fatigue, he completed his seventh dissection.

Ronald was despondent. All that labour down the drain. True, the empty and flaccid stomach tissue of this last of his dissected mosquitoes still remained to be examined. But just then, examining that tissue which spread out like a mosaic courtyard in the miniature seemed like the most futile task. It was going to be another half an hour of futile work and it was difficult to summon the energy to do this. Was it worth it? After all, he had dissected thousands of mosquitoes so far; what use was this one more?

But the 'Angel of Fate', as he called it, laid her hand over his head just then, and hardly had he started his renewed examination of the tissue that he observed a cell with a nearly perfectly circular outline with a diameter of 12 micro metres (1 micro metre = 1/1000000th of a metre). It was obvious to Ronald that the cell was far too small to be an ordinary stomach cell of the mosquito. And then he spotted a couple more identical neighbours.

As he drew more light into the microscope and sharpened the focus, he could see a small cluster of black granules in each of these cells. These granules were shaped like the black pigment granules of the plasmodium crescents of the malarial parasite he had seen earlier in all those human blood smears. Even the count of the number of granules between twelve and sixteen in each cell seemed to correspond with the count found in the malarial parasite found in human blood smears. The suspect had been nailed at last. He had spotted the malarial protozoan in the female dapple-winged variety's salivary glands.

Ronald burst out laughing and shouting and startled his hospital assistant. This was his Eureka moment. In his characteristic modesty, in his diaries, Ronald calls himself 'extremely lucky' to have found both the kind of mosquito that is the actual carrier and the position of the parasite within it in a single day, when in reality he had poured his blood and sweat for years into unfolding the mosquito mystery. He penned the following verse in his diary that day:

'This day designing God
Hath put into my hand
A wondrous thing. And God
Be praised. At His command,
I have found thy secret deeds
Oh mi[ll]ion-murdering Death.
I know that this little thing
A million men will save –
Oh death where is thy sting?
Thy victory oh grave?'[10]

The following day, just to be doubly sure, he dissected the last of the surviving mosquitoes and witnessed the same formation all over again.

On 4 September 1897, he left for Bangalore to join his family, where he wrote a paper on his findings of the previous few months. This paper was published in the *British Medical Journal* on 18 December 1897, and a number of great scientists of the time replicated his results. You just had to catch the right variety and sex of the mosquito – female Anopheles to be precise – cut open its guts, and you were sure to find the same malarial parasites that had been found inside the malarial patients. At last the bureaucracy was moved enough to give him a laboratory to himself in Calcutta, where he tried to carry out the remainder of his work, though not for long.

THE END GAME

What he had found was the key to the mystery. The mystery itself, namely, exactly 'how the mosquitoes infected men, or possibly each other' remained to be open. In other words, exactly how did the malarial parasite travel from mosquito to man? If you think biting is the obvious answer, think again. Flies do not spread cholera by biting. Manson's hypothesis, for instance, was that malaria spread when one consumed parasite-infected water in which mosquitoes had died while laying eggs. So some more work remained to be done before he could verify that malaria was spread by the female Anopheles mosquito by biting, and proving this called for a large sample of humans – not an easy task.

He would need to wait before he could truly pop the cork.

At this point, Ronald was transferred to Rajasthan. Now dry Rajasthan is hardly a place amenable to malarial research. But Ross had never been one to let himself be defeated by such little cards of fate. He had read about bird malaria in the works of Basil

Danielewsky, a Ukrainian expert in avian diseases. He went on to satisfy himself that certain pigeons do carry malaria, even though a number of biologists seemed to believe that birds are immune to malaria. But Ronald studied bird after bird – crows, pigeons, sparrows – and in course proved that mosquitoes do bite birds and that birds are not immune to malaria.

Ronald now needed human volunteers more than ever before to nail the vector's modus operandi beyond all doubt. It was 1898, and with some effort, he managed to have himself transferred once again to Calcutta. He sent one of his local assistants, Mohammad Bux, on an expedition of collecting an assortment of mosquitoes. Bux waded through marshes, sewers, drains, and rotting tanks and brought back a wide spectrum of mosquitoes.

Unable to find human subjects, he turned to the eminently dependable Bux to bring him as many birds – sparrows, crows, pigeons and larks – as he could. He had birds, both infected and healthy, but marked suitably, under fine nets, with mosquitoes for company. Soon he was able to ascertain that the plasmodia do pass from birds to mosquitoes and vice versa, as he was able to spot the same pigmented, circular cellular structure that he was now familiar with, along the stomach walls of the mosquitoes. So there was no reason why the same transfer shouldn't happen with humans. However, the mosquitoes infecting the birds weren't the dapple-winged ones; they were the common household variety. The dapple-winged variety did not spread the infection among birds just as mosquitoes of the common variety did not spread it among humans.

Even though Ronald encountered difficulties in finding enough human subjects to verify his results, he had nevertheless done enough work to conclude that malaria was spread through the female Anopheles mosquito biting humans.

Manson was the first person Ross shared his breakthrough with. He was in the middle of a meeting with the Tropical

Diseases Section of the British Medical Association when a report containing Ross's findings was handed to him. Having read the report, Manson announced to the gathering:

'I am sure you will agree with me that the medical world, I might even say humanity, is extremely indebted to Surgeon Major Ross for what he has already done, and I am sure you will agree with me that every encouragement and assistance should be given to so hard-working, so intelligent, and so successful an investigator to continue his work.'[11]

Alas, encouragement and assistance for Ross as envisaged by Manson didn't come. Such was the inertia of bureaucracy that despite his sterling efforts, he received little support for furthering his work with humans. He was asked to abandon his work on malaria and ordered to report to a new post in Assam to conduct researches on kala-azar! 'Columbus having sighted America was ordered off to discover the North Pole ...'[12] he would remark wryly. Commenting on his superiors, he would observe, '... the man who can do is not allowed to do, because the man who cannot do is put in authority over him.'[13] So disillusioned was he that in 1899 he chose to return to England.

AT LAST, THE HONOURS

Upon returning to England, fame that had eluded Major Ross in India at last came his way. He returned home to join the Liverpool School of Tropical Medicine as a lecturer. The school was commemorating its founder, Sir Alfred Jones. It had collected enough funds to endow a chair in his honour. Ronald Ross was offered the Chair of Tropical Medicine at the University College, which he held from1902 to 1912.

Other recognition and accolades followed. In 1901, he was elected a Fellow of the Royal College of Surgeons of England and a Fellow of the Royal Society. The next year saw him appointed a Companion of the Most Honourable Order of Bath by the king of England.

His earliest tasks after moving to England included investigation and formulation of malaria-prevention programmes in West Africa. He went on to undertake many an excursion to various parts of the world, Egypt (1902), Panama (1904), Greece (1906) and Mauritius (1907-08), to investigate and devise malaria control measures.

Ronald Ross worked tirelessly, contributing to malarial epidemiology as well as to the methods of surveys and assessments of malaria. But his brilliance and ability in connecting dots lay in his applying his mathematical skills picked up very early in life to his observations. He expounded these mathematical models in his sublime work, *Prevention of Malaria*, in 1911. Many of his models were published by the Royal Society in 1915-16. Nor were his mathematical models limited in their scope to epidemiology. Many of his works made significant contributions to pure and applied mathematics, of which the best known are the ones relating to pathometry.

He quantified the economic costs of malaria. His approach remains relevant even today, even if the numbers and percentages have changed over time. He showed with facts and figures that the costs of treating and burying soldiers and civilians were far in excess of what it would cost to prevent malaria. His contempt for penny-pinching politicians and bureaucrats, who could respond only to a prevailing crisis rather than legislate for the future, earned him few friends in the government.

In 1911, he was conferred the Nobel Prize. This was also the year that saw him elevated to the rank of Knight Commander of Bath. Belgium appointed him an Officer in the Order of Leopold II.

Upon leaving Liverpool in 1912, he was appointed the Physician for Tropical Diseases at Kings College Hospital, London. He doubled this position with the Chair of Tropical Sanitation at Liverpool – positions he held till 1917. With World War I well under way, he was appointed Consultant in Malariology to the War Office.

Figure 2: Ross at the luncheon for the thirty-fourth anniversary of Mosquito Day.

His outstanding services in saving a number of soldiers from the scourge of malaria led him to be appointed Knight Commander of the Order of Knight Commander, St Michael and St George, in 1918. He also served as the Malaria Consultant to the Ministry of Pensions.

With his growing fame and influence, it was only a matter of time before his admirers set up a prestigious institution in his honour. The Ross Institute and Hospital of Tropical Diseases and Hygiene was set up in London and Ronald Ross appointed its president for life. He also remained the president of the Society of Tropical Medicine.

In fact, his fame had spread far and wide. There were few countries with scientific culture, inside and outside of Europe, where Ronald had not been honoured for his many contributions.

His was an extraordinary story of the triumph of perspiration over inspiration.

His wife passed away in 1931. Ronald survived her for a year and died after a prolonged illness at the Ross Institute, London, on 16 September 1932.

The story of Ronald Ross – a competent mathematician, sanitarian, epidemiologist, editor, novelist (even if not a particularly good one), dramatist, poet, musician composer and artist – dedicated to the unravelling of the mosquito as the carrier of malaria, is the quintessential story of what scientific temper and scientific methodology is all about. His story is the story of focus, perseverance and dogged pursuit of a goal. It is also a story of the triumph of above-average intelligence combined with hard work over just genius. It is not for nothing that 'the solving of the malaria problem has been called the most dramatic episode in the history of medicine'.[14]

10

Journalist Par Excellence

Mark Tully: The Indian Briton

1935-Alive & Active

KOLKATA, THE ERSTWHILE CALCUTTA, was the capital of colonial India until 1911. The foundation of this great city was laid in the seventeenth century when Emperor Jehangir ruled Delhi. Searching for more profitable trading opportunities in cotton, silk, spices, indigo, salt, tea, opium et al, the East India Company dropped anchor on the eastern shores of the Hooghly river. Several times the English were beaten back, and each time the Company returned doggedly to pursue its trade.

Later, it managed to obtain a firman from Jehangir's son, Emperor Shah Jahan, to set up a factory in Bengal. And Calcutta began to take shape on the banks of the Hooghly – a major distributary of the Ganga, some 265 km long, before it meets the Bay of Bengal. Late in the seventeenth century, the East India

Company obtained an order for permanent presence in Bengal during the governorship of Shaista Khan, under the reign of Shah Jahan's renegade and radical son, Emperor Aurangzeb.

From then on, Calcutta's commercial growth was stupendous and the Bengal Presidency in general and Calcutta city in particular came to acquire a pre-eminent position in the British Empire, not just India. The city grew particularly rapidly in the nineteenth century, when it was hailed as the most important city in the British Empire, second only to London. This was also the time when alongside the development of commerce, the culture in Calcutta also flourished, fusing European philosophies with Indian traditions.

The city would go on to produce revolutionary and progressive thinkers, most of them also committed to the Indian struggle for independence, like Thakur Shri Ramakrishna Paramhamsa, Maa Sarada Devi, Rabindranath Tagore, Swami Vivekananda, Maulana Abul Kalam Azad, Subhas Chandra Bose, Kazi Nazrul Islam, and many others. The city would develop both into a matter of pride as well as pain for the British in more ways than one.

MARK TULLY'S ROOTS

In 1857 – the year of India's first war of independence – a young British soldier found himself in the middle of the uprising in the Eastern United Provinces (present-day Uttar Pradesh). The fellow managed to get away from the scene of action aboard a small boat, in which he travelled down the Ganga all the way to Calcutta. This man was Mark Tully's maternal great-grandfather.

Mark Tully's father was William Scarth Carlisle Tully and his mother was Patience Treby. William Scarth was the first from his Irish family to travel to India. He decided to make his living trading jute in the city. He bought jute in East Bengal (what is now

Bangladesh) and sold it in Calcutta, in West Bengal. A visitor to today's Kolkata, sauntering down the Netaji Subhash Road past BBD Bag, Writer's Building and Lyon's Range, will spot a majestic corner building still carrying the legend: Gillander House. It is probably here that William Scarth worked his way up to a partner in Gillander Arbuthnot, a partnership trading firm of the times, and made it to a director in the Darjeeling Railway. And it is in Calcutta that Mark's mother was born, and where she met William Scarth Carlisle. They were married in St Paul's Cathedral.

Sir William Mark Tully, **or** Tully Saab, was born on 4 October 1935 at 6 Regent Park, Tollygunge (then in the undivided 24 Parganas district) – a sprawling suburb of Calcutta. His birth was registered on 21 November 1935 at the registrar of births, deaths and marriages, Alipore, and he was baptized at the Oxford Mission Church of Behala. He was the second child of the senior Tullys, with four more to follow. All of them would be born in Calcutta – Prudence, Mark, Catherine, Robert, David and Treby – between 1933 and 1944.

William and Patience seem to have been the diehard stiff-upper-lip Brits, with the characteristic attitude of much of the ruling class, for whom India was nothing but a land of natives who had to be looked down their long noses, to preserve their high perch. In this sense, perhaps their attitude was typical of the times. That this was the cultivated attitude in the Tully household would become evident when Mark Tully would state in an interview to the BBC on 19 August 2013: 'From our youngest days, we were never allowed to forget that we were different: we were English, not Indian. We had an English nanny who saw to that. She supervised us 24x7 and once, finding me learning to count from our driver, she cuffed my head, saying "That's the servants' language, not yours".'[1]

In the same interview, Mark Tully recounts that as children he and his siblings were not allowed to play with Indian children. For that matter, they were also expected to be conscious of their class even when playing with European children. For instance, their nanny discouraged them from playing with European children who had Indian or Anglo-Indian nannies, because it was clear that those families could not afford a 'proper (European) nanny', which was what she considered herself. It will perhaps be harsh to view the nanny through the lens of today's way of thinking, given that at the time the Raj presumably 'depended on that image of superiority to enable it to rule so many with so few'.[2] By the 1930s, the foundation of the British Raj in India was beginning to get shaky. The nanny was merely doing her part to prepare the children for the changing times.

Mark Tully would grow up in life not being overly fond of his father, who he claims was a 'stern moralist' with an extremely bad temper to boot.[3] Apparently, Mark's parents maintained a very formal relationship with Mark and his siblings. The Tully children were cared for by their nanny and weren't allowed to meet their parents except twice a day, by appointment.

It must be said here that while India may have suffered from the scourge of the caste system, European society, especially British society, wasn't entirely free of something similar, namely, the class system, which Mark Tully himself alludes to. The British could be said to have been obsessed with class. For instance, the civil servants considered themselves the most superior class – not unlike our brahmins. The army officers came next and considered themselves the warriors or the kshatriya equivalents. Next in the pecking order were the shopkeepers, the traders, or the 'vaisyas', followed by the working classes. While fortunately 'untouchability' had not touched their class system, it was a norm to maintain a healthy social distance from the class below.

The first four years of Mark's life were spent in Calcutta. This would usually be the stage where an English boy would be sent to England for 'proper' education. However, it was now 1939 and the clouds of the Second World War were swirling thick. So Mark was dispatched to Darjeeling for formal schooling. Later, when he was nine and the war was ebbing, he was sent home to England, where he would spend the next twenty-one years.

The first four years of his English schooling were at Twyford School (Hampshire), and then the well-known public high school, Marlborough College.[4] While at Marlborough, he apparently developed a keen interest in theology, which led him to join Lincoln Theological College. He soon switched to Trinity Hall, Cambridge, to study history, having realized a priest's life wasn't for him. He would remark later in life, 'I just knew I could not trust my sexuality to behave as a Christian priest should. And I didn't want to be a cause of scandal.'[5]

A year of Great Britain's National Service later, Mark joined the BBC and in 1965 returned to India at the age of thirty, when India and Pakistan were at war, to start reporting on it immediately. In 1972, the year of the next India-Pakistan war, he was made the BBC bureau chief, a position he maintained for twenty-one years.

It may be said that twenty-one years of midlife in India (plus nine years of childhood), preceded by twenty-one years of formative years in Britain, had made Mark as much an Indian as he may have been a Briton. And by all accounts, including his own, India and its culture had started growing on him.

His Christianity too was beginning to be integrated with various aspects of Hinduism. His one Christian God was introduced to the millions of Hindu Gods, and the patina of India over the Briton that was Mark was complete.

In his initial years in India, as reflected in some of his writings, the conflict of identity – whether he regarded himself a Briton or an Indian – was evident. For example, in *No Full Stops in India*, he refers to himself as 'We, the British … '[6] But in many other contexts, he makes it evident that he loves India and would love to be born in India again, though certainly perhaps not as a poor Indian. In the preface to his book, *The Heart of India*, he writes, there is 'nowhere like India, and no people like Indians'. So clearly Mark Tully must really love India.

But whatever may have been his early inner conflicts of identities, he hardly needs to be awarded a certificate as an India lover. Nothing else can explain the humongous quantities of words he has written on and about India and its people with such deep understanding.

THE BBC YEARS AND AFTER

While with the BBC, Mark covered some of the most important developments in India and South Asia as they were unfolding, including the Indo-Pak conflicts (1965, 1972), Operation Blue Star (1984), the assassination of Indira Gandhi (1984), the anti-Sikh riots in its aftermath, the Bhopal gas disaster (1984), the assassination of Rajiv Gandhi (1991), the demolition of the Babri Masjid (1992) and many other stories all around South Asia.

In 1993, after nearly three decades with the BBC, Mark fell out with its director general of the time, John Birt. He accused Birt of creating a fear psychosis in the BBC, adding 'he could not allow himself to be gagged by the corporation'. Birt returned the compliment to Mark (and along with Mark, scriptwriter Barry Took and broadcaster Sir David Attenborough as well) as 'old soldiers sniping at us with their muskets'.[7]

Mark finally resigned from the BBC in July 1994, commencing a new career as a freelance journalist, and would become a prolific author, apart from making a programme called 'Something Understood' for BBC Radio Four.[8]

As a BBC correspondent, Mark Tully's most notable service to India has been presenting it to the world with dignity and credibility. The dignity and credibility are only enhanced because Mark Tully is not a blind lover and onlooker of India. He loves and sees India in all its colours, in all its shades, with all its warts and moles, through all its ups and downs, its wisdom and follies and its strengths and weaknesses – with the dispassionate attachment of a judge.

By itself, India is a shrill and raucous country, which, even when the right is on its side, or when it is on the side of the right, is not always capable of presenting its case before the world convincingly. It often demands respect when it should be commanding it, and nearly always fails in doing both. It is in this respect that Mark Tully may have rendered his biggest service to India, even if India took a little while to recognize his contribution.

Bringing with him the best of rational Western thinking, a British passport and an Indian heart, he has for long presented the Indian side of the story. It may be that some of the credibility attached to him came from the Raj mantle of 'Tully Sahib' that Mark wore unwittingly – after all, it was an Englishman commenting on India. His love for India is not that of a doting mother for her only child. His adoption of India has been like that of a person who adopts a child knowing full well the ailments which that child may be suffering from but is nevertheless willing to accept it as his very own. He wishes to tell no lies about India, but he wants the world to understand India's challenges better. It is difficult to think of a better ambassador for India. This contribution alone makes Mark Tully worthy of being included among the great British contributors to India who have gone well beyond their call of duty.

Has India fully appreciated his contributions? Perhaps. It did confer upon him the Padma Shri, but not before he had been awarded the Order of the British Empire. India did confer the Padma Bhushan upon him, but not before he was knighted.

Mark Tully's Works

Mark's first book was on India in the aftermath of Operation Blue Star – the army action on the revered Golden Temple in Amritsar against Sikh extremists holed up in the precincts of the holy shrine – and Indira Gandhi's assassination in its wake. It was titled *Amritsar: Mrs Gandhi's Last Battle* (1985) and was co-authored with Satish Jacob, a veteran journalist and author.

His next book was *No Full Stops in India* (1988), an excellent collection of vignettes on the many quirky aspects of India and Indians from a journalist's perspective. The book, published earlier in the US as *The Defeat of a Congressman and Other Parables of Modern India* received some excellent reviews.[9] The *Independent*, for instance, observed: 'His obvious knowledge and love for the country and its people – an affection tempered with a rare objectivity that does not blur his vision to India's poverty or corruption and the contradictions between tradition and modernity … '[10] In the same year, he released another of his books, *Mother*, which was on Mother Teresa.

His only work of fiction, *The Heart of India*, and his first Padma award, the Padma Shri, came in 1995. *The Heart of India* was a collection of his short stories which tried to capture the kaleidoscopic range of many lives that India presents.

Next came *Raj to Rajiv: 40 Years of Indian Independence*, co-authored with Zareer Masani in 1996, based on a BBC radio series that Mark had done earlier under the same title. In the same year were released two more books: *An Investigation into the Lives of Jesus*, to accompany the BBC series of the same title, and published by the BBC (a version of which also came out under the title *Four Faces: A Journey in Search of Jesus the Divine, the Jew, the Rebel, the Sage* in 1997) and *Beyond Purdah*. *Divide and Quit*, co-authored with Penderel Moon (an author and illustrious member of the ICS), was published in 1998 by the Oxford University Press, and it was an authentic account of the pains of the partition of India of 1947.

The Kumbh Mela was released in 2001. The next book, *India in Slow Motion*, co-authored with Gillian Wright, a former BBC colleague and Mark's live-in partner in Delhi, came out in 2002. According to the synopsis written by Penguin India, the publisher, the book explores 'Hindu extremism, child labour, Sufi mysticism, the crisis in agriculture, political corruption and Kashmir' and Mark Tully 'challenges our preconceptions of India – as well as those India has about itself – to create a thoughtful, humorous and deeply profound portrait of a country at odds with itself'. The *Observer* seems to echo the synopsis when it says, 'Few foreigners manage to get under the skin of the world's biggest democracy the way he does, and fewer still can write about it with the clarity and insight he brings to all his work.'[11]

That was also the year Mark Tully was knighted for his many contributions to journalism by the British government.

In 2003, he brought out a compendium titled *Poems to Live By: An Anthology*, co-authored with John Florance, followed by *Last Children of the Raj* (a two-volume set) in 2005. This was also the year Mark Tully received his second Padma award. This was followed by *India's Unending Journey* in 2007.

The year 2010 saw a controversial book from the stables of Roli Books hitting the stands. Published anonymously but widely attributed to Mark – a claim vehemently refuted by him (these authors would like to side with Mark Tully in this regard) – the book was *Hindutva Sex and Adventure*.

In 2011, Mark Tully brought out two more books, *India: The Road Ahead* and *Non-Stop India*.

INDIA FROM MARK'S PERSPECTIVE

Sir William Mark Tully's writings reflect the person that he is: a deep lover of India. 'There is nowhere like India and no people like Indians,' he says. And yet, he is intimately familiar with every fault and blemish of India and Indians. Having spent nearly half a century in India, Mark not only understands India intimately, but he is also decidedly an Indian at heart. However, with his impressionable years having been spent in Britain, and having retained his British passport all these years (India does not allow dual citizenships), he also harbours a spacious corner for Britain in the same heart. As an Indian, he 'believes' in karma and says his 'karma was to be born a British – and you can't lose that'. Thus he is both an insider and an outsider to India, though perhaps more on the inside than outside. He loves India enough not to call it a failing state, but he is rational enough to call it a flailing state.

One can get a clear idea of Mark Tully's perspective and understanding of India through two of his major works: *No Full Stops in India* and *The Heart of India*.

While *The Heart of India* is a collection of real stories from the lives of people, *No Full Stops in India* is an exploration, based on real experiences, of the chaotic democracy that Indian politics represents and the myriad social challenges that make India as the country struggles to modernize. He draws an elegant portrait of the 2,000 years of anthropology that India simultaneously presents on a narrow stretch of road. He provides many examples of perennial conflicts between modernity and tradition, especially in rural India, like the effect of buses, cars and three-wheeler autos on the life of an ikka-wallah (or a horse-cart driver), or the effect of stainless steel, plastic and ceramic on the life of a clay-potter.

If one weren't careful, one could mistake Mark Tully's bemoaning the tragedy modernity brings in the lives of those affected by it as a call against modernity. But perhaps that is not his intent at all. He is a modern man and is not under the illusion that change is a painless process. He simply explores the flip side of this human tragedy in a telling manner, which can serve to sensitize pro-modernists to the fact that their prosperity does not come without a heavy price.

The work highlights the feudal society that India continues to be. Nor is he blind to the sufferings of the well-off. He writes with empathy of the sufferings of the zamindars or the landlords in the aftermath of the abolition of the zamindari system. He comments on how the caste system comes in the way of economic prosperity, because people from the higher castes would not deign to indulge in what they consider to be the trades of the lower ones. The book also contains segments commenting on the changing nature and role of religion in India. He is undeniably influenced by the Hindu way of life and positions himself somewhere midway between Christianity and Hinduism.

All in all, Tully's *No Full Stops in India* – which takes a dispassionate look at a multitude of aspects that make India – is an empathetic book that scores over both V.S. Naipual's *India: A Wounded Civilization* or V. Raghunathan's *Games Indians Play* – both of which merely hold a mirror to the ugliness of India, albeit in their own different ways.

His work with BBC Radio Four is more esoteric. About his programme 'Something Understood', he says in an interview, 'It's a discussion about matters which you cannot understand fully, such as philosophy, poetry, religion, all sorts of things, but less in the rational field and more in the intuition field.'

On religion in India, he observes in the same interview, echoing the thoughts also reflected in some of his books, 'I think Indians on average take religion much more seriously than people do in the UK. They are more observant of religions. Religion is a great spiritual tradition in India and I believe that tradition is very much still alive, and I don't think it's been lost – but the fear is that it will be. I think the culture has been preserved to an extent; but unbridled materialism, capitalism and consumerism is bound to undermine it. My appeal in *India's Unending Journey* is that these things [not] be taken too far and there should be a middle road between government control, socialism and capitalism. You must look at the negatives of economic growth too, the most obvious being the environment.'

His deep understanding of India is also evident in his journalistic works. Most reviewers of his works seem to acknowledge that Mark does not suffer from the typical bias of the Westerner against India and Indians.

As a BBC correspondent operating from Delhi, he has not only enjoyed high visibility in India, he has also been at a vantage point from where he could observe the country in better relief than most. His years of broadcasting on the much respected BBC Radio, which represented fair reporting in India for decades, enabled him to reach every nook and cranny of India – rural and urban alike.

This also brought him a high degree of recognition along the length and breadth of India. His deep commitment to understanding Indian issues and the manner of his reporting, for instance, the Indo-Pak wars, also earned him a high degree of credibility among Indians. There was a time when an average Indian would find the words of Mark Tully on the BBC more reliable than the government-controlled All India Radio.

And yet, India is a land of contradictions. Notwithstanding his reputation for credibility, it is not as if Mark Tully has not had to pay a price for his unbiased reporting from time to time. Indira Gandhi wasn't too enamoured with his upright reporting of her declaration of internal emergency and had him expelled in 1975. Following his reporting of the storming of the Babri Masjid, he was 'chased by a howling mob and then trapped in a tiny room for two hours'. He had to escape 'disguised in a long shawl – only to be denounced a few days later by the Indian government and police officials for broadcasting the truth about the resulting riots and political crisis'. 'We were surrounded by a huge mob screaming, "Death to Mark Tully!" and "Death to BBC!"' he would recall with a grin to the *Los Angeles Times* in 1992.[12]

MARK – THE MAN

Like his duality of nationalities at heart, he is a public and a private person at the same time. Google Mark Tully and you find no less than 8.5 million results. He is all over the web space. And yet, try finding some intimate details about how well he did in school, or when and where he met his wife, or exactly when and where he got married, when and where his children were born, or what their names are, and so forth, you find he is not such a public persona after all. Nor does he have a biography one can fall back on. He even states in one of his books that he has never thought of writing an autobiography because he does not want to give the impression that his life is particularly important.[13]

But if you are persistent, you figure out that his wife Margaret lives in London with his four children – Emma, Serra, Sam and Patrick – all born before 1969 but not necessarily in that order. You also find that while he lives with Margaret when in England, he lives with his partner of thirty years, Gillian Wright, a former BBC colleague, when in Delhi.[14]

Of his mother Patience Terby we know little except that as late as 2001 she lived in Delhi not far from Mark, though she passed away in the 2000s. Nor do we know too much about his children. We do know from one of his recent interviews that he is a proud grandfather of ten.[15] We also know that his elder son Sam is married to Nandita, an Indian banker in London, and Aditya, their son, whom Mark refers to as Anglo-Indian, is the youngest of his grandchildren.

In 2013, at the age of seventy-eight, Mark Tully made news when applying for the status of Oversees Citizen of India, when he suddenly needed to get proof of his birth from Kolkata. Fortunately, he got his certificate, after some initial hiccups, in November 2013 – about the time this chapter was being written.

Figure 1: Sir Tully with his children in the 1970s.

Even today, Sir Tully remains the cultured and courteous British-Indian that he has always been. He has opinions on virtually every aspect of India, though he is hardly opinionated. His journalism has been of the highest standards – impartial and yet with a distinct compassion for India and Indians. His books provide an objective commentary on India over four decades – the good, the bad and the ugly – but not without some underlying empathy throughout.

Perhaps it is the generous dash of the Briton – the Tully Sahib part – in him that makes his understanding of India a tad more complete, a tad more correct and a tad more courageous than would have been possible for a 100 per cent Indian. He is the best bridge a complex India could have hoped for between itself and the West.

More important, perhaps, Tully's BBC World Service dispatches – first broadcast in English and then rebroadcast in Hindi, Urdu, Tamil, Nepali and Bengali – are the most reliable source of unfiltered, uncensored news about major events for millions in India, Pakistan and Bangladesh.

Mark Tully has an indelible place as the most popular and loved Englishman in contemporary India, a love that he reciprocates in equal measure.

Notes

Introduction

1. Charles C. Mann, 'How the Potato Changed the World', *Smithsonian Magazine*, accessed 16 July 2014, http://www.smithsonianmag.com/history/how-the-potato-changed-the-world-108470605/.
2. http://www.britannica.com/oscar/article-9031775; also see George P. Landow, accessed 9 July 2014, http://www.victorianweb.org/history/empire/india/eic.html.
3. Adrian Lee, 'The Remarkable Raj: Why Britain should be proud of its rule in India', *Express*, 22 June 2013, accessed 10 July 2014, http://www.express.co.uk/news/uk/409374/The-Remarkable-Raj-Why-Britain-should-be-proud-of-its-rule-in-India.

Chapter 1

1. John Aikin, *Select Works of the British Poets: In a Chronological Series from...* (London: Mathew & Leigh, 1812), 52.
2. Henry Malden, *Distinguished Men of Modern Times, Vol. II* (New York: Harper & Brothers, 1842), 194.
3. *The West Minster Review, Vol. 106-107* (1876): 200.
4. Henry Roscoe Esq^R, *Eminent British Lawyers* (London: Longman, Rees, Orme, Brown & Green, Pattermoster Row, 1830), 328.
5. Ibid.
6. As quoted in: Marco Wan, ed., *Reading the Legal Case: Cross Currents between Law and the Humanities, a Glass House Book* (New York: Routledge, 2012), 82. The reference can also be found in: Major M.H. Court, M.R.A.S., *The Future Government of India: Considered in Its*

Relation to a Compact With Its Native Subjects (London: W.M.H. Allen & Co., 1858), 37.

7. Cited from Michael J. Franklin, ed., *Sir William Jones: Selected Poetical and Prose Works* (Cardiff: University of Wales Press, 1995), 355-70. Also: Winfred P. Lehmann, *A Reader in Nineteenth Century Historical Indo-European Linguistics* (Bloomington: Indiana University Press, 1967).

8. Sir William Jones, *Graves Chamney Haughton (Translated)* (London: W.M.H. Allen & Co., 1869) (available online).

Websites referred:

http://www.asiaticsoceitycal.com, accessed 12 July 2009

http://asiaticsocietycal.com/library/index.htm, accessed 12 July 2009

http://en.wikipedia.org/wiki/Wales, accessed 15 July 2009

http://www.anglesey-history.co.uk/anghist.html, accessed 15 July 2009

http://en.wikipedia.org/wiki/History_of_mathematics#17th_century, accessed 15 July 2009

http://en.wikipedia.org/wiki/Llanfechell, accessed 15 July 2009

http://en.wikipedia.org/wiki/William_Jones_(mathematician), accessed 26 December 2013

http://books.google.co.in/books/about/A_New_Compendium_of_the_Whole_Art_of_Pra.html?id=Gm9bAAAAQAAJ&redir_esc=y, accessed 26 December 2013

http://www.distances from.com/gb/Anglesey-latitude-longitude-Anglesey-latitude-Anglesey-longitude/LatLongHistory/617344.aspx, accessed 26 December 2013

http://www-history.mcs.st-andrews.ac.uk/Printonly/Jones.html, accessed 15 July 2009

http://en.wikipedia.org/wiki/William_Jones_(mathematician), accessed 17 July 2009

http://en.wikipedia.org/wiki/Thomas_Parker,_1st_Earl_of_Macclesfield, accessed 17 July 2009

http://www.notablebiographies.com/supp/Supplement-Fl-Ka/Jones-William.html, accessed 20 July 2009

http://www.theodora.com/encyclopedia/j/sir_william_jones.html, accessed 24 December 2013

http://encyclopedia.jrank.org/JEE_JUN/JONES_SIR_WILLIAM_1746_1794_.html, accessed 24 December 2013 http://en.wikipedia.org/wiki/Mu'allaqat, accessed 24 December 2013

http://en.wikisource.org/wiki/1911_Encyclop%C3%A6dia_Britannica/
   Calcutta, accessed 26 December 2013

http://en.wikipedia.org/wiki/Asiatic_Society_of_Mumbai, accessed 26
   December 2013

http://en.wikipedia.org/wiki/Manusm%E1%B9%9Bti, accessed 22 July
   2009

http://encyclopedia.jrank.org/JEE_JUN/JONES_SIR_
   WILLIAM_1746_1794_.html, accessed 22 July 2009

http://wbo.llgc.org.uk/en/s-JONE-WIL-1675.html, accessed 22 July 2009

CHAPTER 2

1. Francis Tucker, *The Yellow Scarf* (London: J.M. Dent, 1961),
    2, accessed 22 November 2013, http://books.google.co.in/
    books?id=qRQiHNIaEuYC.
2. William Henry Sleeman, *Rambles and Recollections of an Indian
    Official, Vol. 1* (1844): 2, accessed 22 November 2013, http://books.
    google.co.in/books?id=DZMtAAAAMAAJ.
3. Ibid, 27.
4. Ibid.
5. Ibid, 28.
6. Ibid, 30.
7. Máire ní Fhlathúin, 'That Solitary Englishman: W.H. Sleeman and
    the Biography of British India', accessed 22 November 2013, http://
    eprints.nottingham.ac.uk/1984/1/biography_victorian_review_2001.
    pdf.
8. Vijai Shukul, 'Sleeman Sahib Ki Jai', in *The Indian Police Journal*,
    October-December, 2012, Vol. LIX, 4, accessed 22 November 2013,
    http://www.bprd.nic.in/writereaddata/mainlinkFile/File1052.pdf.
9. Francis Tucker, *The Yellow Scarf* (London: J.M. Dent, 1961),
    93, accessed 22 November 2013, http://books.google.co.in/
    books?id=qRQiHNIaEuYC.
10. William Henry Sleeman, *Rambles and Recollections of an Indian
    Official, Vol. 1* (1844): 317, accessed 22 November 2013, http://books.
    google.co.in/books?id=DZMtAAAAMAAJ.
11. Vijai Shukul, 'Sleeman Sahib Ki Jai', in *The Indian Police Journal*,
    October-December, 2012, Vol. LIX, 4, accessed 22 November 2013,

http://www.bprd.nic.in/writereaddata/mainlinkFile/File1052.pdf.

12. William Henry Sleeman, *Rambles and Recollections of an Indian Official, Vol. 1* (1844): 188, accessed 22 November 2013, http://books. google.co.in/books?id=DZMtAAAAMAAJ.

13. Ibid, 190. Also see the interview in the e-magazine 'Knowledge @ Wharton' of Wharton Business School at http://knowledge.wharton. upenn.edu/article/v-raghunathan-indians-are-privately-smart-and-publicly-dumb/.

14. Vijai Shukul, 'Sleeman Sahib Ki Jai', in *The Indian Police Journal, October-December, 2012, Vol. LIX,* 4, accessed 22 November 2013, http://www.bprd.nic.in/writereaddata/mainlinkFile/File1052.pdf.

15. William Henry Sleeman, *Rambles and Recollections of an Indian Official, Vol. 1* (1844): 128, accessed 22 November 2013, http://books. google.co.in/books?id=DZMtAAAAMAAJ.

16. Francis Tucker, *The Yellow Scarf* (London: J.M. Dent, 1961), ix, accessed 22 November 2013, http://books.google.co.in/ books?id=qRQiHNIaEuYC.

Websites referred:

http://en.wikipedia.org/wiki/William_Henry_Sleeman, accessed 22 November 2013.

http://www.damninteresting.com/the-thugs-of-india/, accessed 3 December 2013.

https://nathanmohr.wordpress.com/tag/william-sleeman/, accessed 3 December 2013.

http://en.wikisource.org/wiki/Sleeman,_William_Henry_(DNB00) , accessed 22 November 2013.

http://wikimapia.org/13680580/Major-William-Henry-Sleeman-s-Reformatory-School-Durrie-Khana, accessed 22 November 2013.

http://www.geocities.ws/rampalr1/sleemanindia.htm, accessed 22 November 2013.

http://www.jabalpur.nic.in/heritage/discover%20jabalpur.pdf, accessed 22 November 2013.

http://www-personal.umich.edu/~wilsonja/Titanosauria/Background.html, accessed 5 December 2013.

http://2ndlook.wordpress.com/2011/07/05/how-british-raj-ended-thugee-in-india/, accessed 3 December 2013.

Image credits:

Figure 1: Courtesy Vijai Shukul, additional director general of police (retd), Madhya Pradesh.

Figure 2: Courtesy Pradeep Singh, additional general manager (mobile), Bharat Sanchar Nigam Limited 'http://www.panoramio.com/photo/54591161, accessed 6 June 2014.

CHAPTER 3

1. Thomas Babbington Macaulay, *Macaulay's Essays on Clive and Hastings* (Boston: Ginn and Company, 1910), 209-210, accessed 20 February 2014, http://www.forgottenbooks.org/readbook_text/Macaulays_Essays_on_Clive_and_Hastings_1000275193/209.

2. John Francis Davis, *Vizier Ali Khan; Or, The Massacre of Benares: A Chapter in British Indian History* (London: Spottiswoode & Co, 1871), 14, accessed 14 February 2014, https://archive.org/details/vizieralikhanor00davigoog.

3. Thomas Edward Colebrooke, *Life of the Honourable Mountstuart Elphinstone* (New York: Cambridge University Press, 2011), 9, accessed 20 February 2014, https://books.google.co.in/books?id=tSoMEJ-_Nx 0C&printsec=frontcover&dq=isbn:1108097227&hl=en&sa=X&ei= SydnVaXeLYaouwSgo4OQAg&ved=0CB0Q6AEwAA#v=onepage&q &f=false.

4. Ibid, 14.

5. Avril Ann Powell, *Scottish Orientalists and India: The Muir Brothers, Religion, Education and Empire* (Woodbridge: Boydell & Brewer, 2010), 7, accessed 28 May 2015, https://books.google.co.in/books?i d=KOnS1X8a528C&printsec=frontcover&source=gbs_ge_summary _r&cad=0#v=onepage&q&f=false.

6. Ibid.

7. Major B.D. Basu, 'History of Education in India under the Rule of the East India Company', *The Modern Review Office* (1867), accessed 10 December 2014, https://archive.org/details/historyofeducati034991mbp.

8. 'Court of Directors' Public Department Despatch to the Governor-General in Council of Fort William in Bengal', 3 June 1814, accessed 10 December 2013, https://archive.org/details/historyofeducati034991mbp.

9. 'Elphinstone's Minute on Education', accessed 10 December 2013, http://www.sdstate.edu/projectsouthasia/loader.cfm?csModule=security/getfile&PageID=854226.

10. James Sutherland Cotton, *Mountstuart Elphinstone and the Making of South-Western India* (Oxford: Clarendon press, 1911), 187, accessed 10 December 2013, http://archive.org/stream/mountstuartelphi00cott/mountstuartelphi00cott_djvu.txt.

11. Ibid, 190.

12. H.R. James, *Education and Statesmanship in India* (London: Longmans, Green, and Co., 1911), 129, accessed 22 December 2013, http://archive.org/stream/educationandstat035007mbp/educationandstat035007mbp_djvu.txt.

13. Charles Macfarlane, *Reminiscences of a Literary Life* (New York: C. Scribner's Sons, 1917), 166-167, accessed 10 December 2013, https://archive.org/stream/reminiscencesal00macfgoog/reminiscencesal00macfgoog_djvu.txt.

14. James Sutherland Cotton, *Mountstuart Elphinstone and the Making of South-Western India* (Oxford: Clarendon press, 1911), 191, accessed 10 December 2013, http://archive.org/stream/mountstuartelphi00cott/mountstuartelphi00cott_djvu.txt.

Websites referred:

http://www.britannica.com/EBchecked/topic/185289/Mountstuart-Elphinstone, accessed 10 December 2013.

http://en.wikipedia.org/wiki/Mountstuart_Elphinstone, accessed 10 December 2013.

http://archive.spectator.co.uk/article/3rd-may-1884/20/mountstuart-elphinstone-we-are-very-glad-to-see-am, accessed 10 December 2013.

http://www.electricscotland.com/history/india/page5.htm, accessed 3 January 2014.

http://www-personal.une.edu.au/~hbrasted/kipling/topic02.html, accessed 10 December 2013.

http://www.iranicaonline.org/articles/elphinstone, accessed 10 December 2013.

Chapter 4

1. http://www.historyofparliamentonline.org/volume/1790-1820/

member/prinsep-john-1746-1831, accessed 28 December, 2014.

2. Ajay Mitra Shastri, 'James Prinsep and Study of Early Indian History', *Annals of the Bhandarkar Oriental Research Institute, Vol. 80, No. 1/4* (1999).

3. James Prinsep, 'Description of a Compensation Barometer, and Observations on Wet Barometers', *Journal of the Asiatic Society of Bengal,* 2 (1833): 258-262.

4. James Prinsep, 'Experiments on the Preservation of Sheet Iron from Rust in India', *Journal of the Asiatic Society of Bengal,* 3 (1834): 191-192.

5. James Prinsep, 'On the Measurement of High Temperatures', *Philosophical Transactions of the Royal Society of London, 118* (1828): 79-95.

6. James Prinsep, ed., 'The Balloon', *The Journal of the Asiatic Society of Bengal, Vol. V* (1836): 255.

Websites referred:

http://en.wikipedia.org/wiki/Prinsep, accessed 26 December 2013

http://www.historyofparliamentonline.org/volume/1790-1820/member/prinsep-john-1746-1831, accessed 26 December 2013

http://en.wikipedia.org/wiki/James_Prinsep, accessed 26 December 2013

http://www.britannica.com/EBchecked/topic/476995/James-Prinsep, accessed 26 December 2013

http://www.tribuneindia.com/2010/20100328/spectrum/main2.htm, accessed 26 December 2013

http://rahugho.blogspot.in/2010/02/james-prinsep.html, accessed 28 December 2013

Image credits:

Figure 1: Picture courtesy: The Asiatic Society, Calcutta, as reproduced in P. Thankappan Nair, *James Prinsep: Life and Work Volume One* (Firma KLM Private Limited, 1999).

Figure 2: Picture courtesy: The Asiatic Society, Calcutta, as reproduced in P. Thankappan Nair, *James Prinsep: Life and Work Volume One* (Firma KLM Private Limited, 1999).

Figure 3: Wikimedia Commons, accessed 2 June 2014, http://commons.wikimedia.org/wiki/File:James_Prinsep.jpg

Chapter 5

1. Lady Hope, *General Sir Arthur Cotton: His Life and Works* (New Delhi: Asiatic Education Services, 2005), 12.
2. Ibid, 14.
3. Bret Wallach, 'Irrigation in British India', in *Losing Asia, Modernization and the Culture of Development* (Baltimore: Johns Hopkins University Press, 1996), 57, accessed 30 December 2013, http://parker. ou.edu/~bwallach/documents/Losing%20Asia%20-%20Ch%204.pdf.
4. Uma Maheshwari, 'The Empire Flows Again', India Together, 2 June 2009, accessed 31 December 2013, http://www.indiatogether.org/2009/jun/env-cotton.htm.
5. Gautam R. Desiraju, 'Letter to the editor', *Current Science, Vol. 85, No. 3* (2003): 236.
6. 'Sir Arthur Cotton anicut partially damaged', *The Hindu*, 1 November 2012.
7. Uma Maheshwari, 'The Empire Flows Again', India Together, 2 June 2009, accessed 31 December 2013, http://www.indiatogether.org/2009/jun/env-cotton.htm.
8. Christopher V. Hill, *South Asia: An Environmental History* (California: ABC-CLIO Inc., 2008), 129.
9. Uma Maheshwari, 'The Empire Flows Again', India Together, 2 June 2009, accessed 31 December 2013, http://www.indiatogether.org/2009/jun/env-cotton.htm.
10. Lady Hope, *General Sir Arthur Cotton: His Life and Works* (New Delhi: Asiatic Education Services, 2005), 12.
11. Bret Wallach, 'Irrigation in British India', in *Losing Asia, Modernization and the Culture of Development* (Baltimore: Johns Hopkins University Press, 1996), 59, accessed 30 December 2013, http://parker. ou.edu/~bwallach/documents/Losing%20Asia%20-%20Ch%204.pdf.

Websites referred:

http://en.wikipedia.org/wiki/Arthur_Cotton, accessed 15 February 2010
http://encyclopedia.jrank.org/SHA_SIV/SIR_ARTHUR_THOMAS_COTTON_1803_1.html, accessed 15 February 2010
http://en.wikipedia.org/wiki/Arthur_Cotton, accessed 15 February 2010
http://www.britannica.com/EBchecked/topic/139892/Sir-Arthur-Thomas-Cotton, accessed 15 February 2010

http://www.nationmaster.com/encyclopedia/Sir-Arthur-Cotton, accessed 20 February 2010

http://www.absoluteastronomy.com/topics/Grand_Anicut, accessed 12 June 2011

CHAPTER 6

1. L.S.S. O'Malley, *Bengal District Gazetteer: Darjeeling* (New Delhi: Logos Press, 1999)), 190, accessed 10 January 2014, http://books. google.co.in/books?id=LhOzszXcM9UC.

2. Ibid, 21.

3. *The Journal of the Anthropological Institute of Great Britain and Ireland, Vol. 7* (1878): 382, accessed 10 January 2014, http://www. jstor.org/discover/10.2307/2841015?uid=3738256&uid=2&uid=4& sid=21103203117267.

4. Nandini Bhattacharya, *Contagion and Enclaves: Tropical Medicine in Colonial India* (Liverpool: Liverpool University Press, 2012), 24, accessed 10 January 2014, http://books.google.co.in/ books?id=49B1d1e6aTsC.

5. Joseph Dalton Hooker, *Himalayan Journals, Vol. 2* (1855), 175, accessed 10 January 2014, http://www.gutenberg.org/cache/epub/6477/ pg6477.html.

6. *The Journal of the Anthropological Institute of Great Britain and Ireland Vol. 7* (1878): 379-91, accessed 10 January 2014, http://www. jstor.org/discover/10.2307/2841015?uid=3738256&uid=2&uid=4& sid=21103203117267.

7. *The Journal of the Anthropological Institute of Great Britain and Ireland Vol. 7* (1878): 382, accessed 10 January 2014, http://www. jstor.org/discover/10.2307/2841015?uid=3738256&uid=2&uid=4& sid=21103203117267.

8. L.S.S. O'Malley, *Bengal District Gazetteer: Darjeeling* (New Delhi: Logos Press, 1999), 28, accessed 10 January 2014, http://books.google. co.in/books?id=LhOzszXcM9UC.

9. http://www.wipo.int/ipadvantage/en/details.jsp?id=2540, accessed 15 January 2014.

10. http://www.darjeeling-tourism.com/darj_0000bd.htm, accessed 15 January 2014.

11. *The Journal of the Anthropological Institute of Great Britain and*

Ireland Vol. 7 (1878): 382, accessed 10 January 2014, http://www.
jstor.org/discover/10.2307/2841015?uid=3738256&uid=2&uid=4&
sid=21103203117267.

12. Ibid, 382.
13. Ibid, 382.
14. Ibid, 382.
15. Nandini Bhattacharya, 'Leisure, Economy and Colonial Urbanism: Darjeeling, 1835–1930', in the *Journal of Urban History*, accessed 10 January 2014, http://www.ncbi.nlm.nih.gov/pmc/articles/PMC3837203/.
16. http://www.nepjol.info/index.php/HN/article/viewFile/7104/5766, accessed 12 January 2014.
17. Joseph Dalton, *Portraits of the Himalayas*, (Leicester: Troubadour, 2006), 234-35, accessed 31 January 2014, http://books.google.co.in/books?id=fFVFA5fIrAsC&pg=PA235&lpg=PA235#v=onepage&q&f=false.
18. http://www.botanic.co.uk/pages/CoolplantFebruarius, accessed 12 January 2014.

Websites referred:

http://www.ndsu.edu/pubweb/~rcollins/travel/darjeelingtea.html, accessed 12 January 2014.

http://darjeeling.gov.in/darj-hist.html, accessed 12 January 2014.

http://en.wikipedia.org/wiki/History_of_Darjeeling, accessed 13 January 2014.

http://www.jdhooker.org.uk/biography4.htm, accessed 12 January 2014.

http://happyearthtea.com/blogs/tea-101/7904251-history-of-darjeeling-tea, accessed 15 March 2014.

http://indiatoday.intoday.in/story/things-that-make-india-proud-darjeeling-tea/1/218950.html, accessed 15 March 2014.

http://indian-heritage-and-culture.blogspot.in/2012/12/darjeeling-view-from-beechwood-vintage.html, accessed 12 April 2014.

http://www.ndsu.edu/pubweb/~rcollins/travel/darjeelingtea.html, accessed 17 April 2014.

http://www.teagenius.com/index.php?option=com_content&view=article&id= 72:the-history-of-darjeeling-tea&catid=27&Itemid=119, accessed 17 April 2014.

http://www.artofeating.com/tt/darjeeling.htm, accessed 17 April 2014.

http://www.wipo.int/ipadvantage/en/details.jsp?id=2540, accessed 17 April 2014.

http://darjeelingtealovers.com/growing_conditions.php, accessed 15 April 2014.

http://www.darjeeling-tourism.com/darj_0000bd.htm, accessed 15 April 2014.

http://www.botanic.co.uk/pages/CoolplantFebruarius, accessed 15 April 2014.

http://theteadetective.com/IndiaTeaGrowsDarjeeling.html, accessed 15 April 2014.

http://darjeeling.gov.in/darj-tea.html, accessed 15 April 2014.

http://tourismofdarjeeling.blogspot.in/2010/06/darjeeling-tea-garden-darjeeling-tea.html, accessed 15 April 2014.

http://www.teauction.com/home/heritage.asp, accessed 15 April 2014.

http://www.crommelin.org/history/Biographies/1763CharlesRussel/Part3/03-CharlesRussel.htm, accessed 15 April 2014.

Image credits:

Figure 1: By kind courtesy of Dokka Srinivasu, from his personal collection of vintage postcards. Accessed 12 April 2014, http://indian-heritage-and-culture.blogspot.in/2012/12/darjeeling-view-from-beechwood-vintage.html.

CHAPTER 7

1. 'The World's Highway – A Proposal to Construct a Railway Running between Calcutta and London', in *The Calcutta Review*, 8, accessed 10 March 2014, http://books.google.co.in/books/reader?id=q3ABAAAAQAAJ.

2. 'London to Calcutta in a Week', in the *New Zealand Herald, Vol. XX, Issue 6859*, accessed 10 March 2014, http://paperspast.natlib.govt.nz/cgi-bin/paperspast?a=d&d=NZH18831110.2.56.22.

3. Blair B. Kling, *Partner in Empire: Dwarkanath Tagore and the Age of Enterprise in Eastern India* (Berkeley: University of California Press, 1976), 190, accessed 10 March 2014, http://books.google.co.in/books?id=KVBKeqaYeVwC.

4. Anuradha Kumar, 'Two Men and a Railway Line', Indian Railways

Fan Club Association, accessed 10 March 2014, http://www.irfca.org/articles/two-men-railway-line.html.

5. G. Huddleston, *History of the East Indian Railway* (Calcutta: Thacker, Spink & Co., 1906), 10, accessed 10 March 2014, https://archive.org/stream/historyeastindi00huddgoog#page/n8/mode/2up.

6. John Chapman, 'Principles of Indian Reform: Being Brief Hints, Together with a Plan for the Improvement of the Constituency of the East India Company, and for the Promotion of Indian Public Works', (London: John Chapman, 1853), 12, accessed 23 April 2014, https://play.google.com/books/reader?id=NCNYAAAAcAAJ&printsec=frontcover&output=reader&authuser=0&hl=en&pg=GBS.PA13.

7. Ralf Roth and Günter Dinhobl, ed., 'John Chapman and the Great Indian Peninsula Railway', in *Across the Borders: Financing the World's Railways in the Nineteenth and Twentieth Centuries* (Cornwall: Ashgate, 2008), 237, accessed 10 March 2014, http://railwayengineering.in/wp-content/uploads/2013/05/John-Chapman-and-the-Promotion-of-the-Great-Indian-Peninsula-Railway.pdf Ian J. Kerr.

8. Ibid, 237.

9. Jennet Humphreys, *Dictionary of National Biography, 1885-1900, Vol. 10*, accessed 11 April 2014, http://en.wikisource.org/wiki/Chapman,_John_(1801-1854)_(DNB00).

10. 'The First Train in India', Indian Railways Fan Club Association, accessed 10 March 2014, http://irfca.org/docs//history/au-news-gipr-first-train-1853.html.

11. Christian Wolmar, *Blood, Iron and Gold: How the Railways Transformed the World*, (London: Atlantic Books, 2009), accessed 3 November 2013, http://books.google.co.in/books?id=kGJUzEA3T4YC.

12. 'Extracts from Australian Newspapers', Indian Railways Fan Club Association, accessed 10 March 2014, http://irfca.org/docs/history/au-news-gipr-first-train-1853.html.

13. 'Extracts from the Railway Times', Indian Railways Fan Club Association, http://irfca.org/docs/history/railway-times.html.

14. Trove Digitised Newspapers, accessed 21 October 2013, http://trove.nla.gov.au/ndp/del/article/12969728?searchTerm=Indian+Railways.

15. G. Huddleston, *History of the East Indian Railway* (Calcutta: Thacker, Spink & Co., 1906), 17, accessed 27 May 2015, https://archive.org/stream/historyeastindi00huddgoog#page/n8/mode/2up.

16. Christian Wolmar, *Blood, Iron and Gold: How the Railways Transformed the World* (London: Atlantic Books, 2009), accessed 3 November 2013, http://books.google.co.in/books?id=kGJUzEA3T4YC.

17. Christian Wolmar, *Blood, Iron and Gold: How the Railways Transformed the World* (London: Atlantic Books, 2009), accessed 3 November 2013, http://books.google.co.in/books?id=kGJUzEA3T4YC.

18. Grace's Guide, accessed 21 October 2013, http://www.gracesguide.co.uk/Rowland_Macdonald_Stephenson.

19. Trove Digitised Newspapers, accessed 21 October 2013, http://trove.nla.gov.au/ndp/del/article/12969728?searchTerm=Indian+Railways.

Websites referred:

http://www.essaysinhistory.com/articles/2011/5, accessed 10 March 2014.

http://www.historyofparliamentonline.org/volume/1820-1832/member/stephenson-rowland-1782-1856, accessed 10 March 2014.

http://ftfmagazine.lewcock.net/index.php?option=com_content&view=article&id=198:road-rail-and-air-transport-pioneer&catid=46:march-2009, accessed 11 March 2014.

http://www.columbia.edu/itc/mealac/pritchett/00routesdata/1800_1899/britishrule/railways/railways.html, accessed 11 March 2014.

http://www.hindu.com/thehindu/mp/2002/04/18/stories/2002041800430100.htm, accessed 23 April 2014.

http://ibnlive.in.com/news/vintage-images-160-years-of-indias-first-passenger-train-journey/385681-3.html, accessed 10 March 2014.

http://irfca.org/docs/history/india-first-railways.html, accessed 11 March 2014.

http://irfca.org/docs//history/au-news-official-resistance-railway.html, accessed 11 March 2014.

http://www.gracesguide.co.uk/Rowland_Macdonald_Stephenson, accessed 11 March 2014.

http://nzetc.victoria.ac.nz/tm/scholarly/tei-Gov04_07Rail-t1-body-d10.html, accessed 11 March 2014.

http://www.irfca.org/articles/two-men-railway-line.html, accessed 11 March 2014.

Image credits:

Figure 1: 'Bombay Photo Images', accessed 24 July 2014, http://oldphotosbombay.blogspot.in/2013/06/blog-post.html.

Figure 2: Indian Railways Fan Club Association, owner: Harsh Vardhan, accessed 24 July 2014, http://www.irfca.org/gallery/Heritage/orion+-+EIR.bmp.html.

Figure 3: The Graphic Illustrated Weekly Magazine, courtesy Dr Frances Pritchett, professor of South Asian literature, Columbia University.

CHAPTER 8

1. Joseph Davey Cunningham, *The History of the Sikhs* (London: J. Murray, 1853), 279, accessed 27 November 2013, https://archive.org/details/historyofthesikh025030mbp.

2. Col G.B. Malleson, *The Decisive Battles of India* (London: W.H. Allen & Co., 1885), xxiv, accessed 27 November 2013, http://archive.org/stream/decisivebattleso00malluoft/decisivebattleso00malluoft_djvu.txt.

3. Joseph Davey Cunningham, *The History of the Sikhs* (London: J. Murray, 1853), xxi, accessed 27 November 2013, https://archive.org/details/historyofthesikh025030mbp.

4. Col G.B. Malleson, *The Decisive Battles of India* (London: W.H. Allen & Co., 1885), xxiv, accessed 27 November 2013, http://archive.org/stream/decisivebattleso00malluoft/decisivebattleso00malluoft_djvu.txt.

5. Evans Bell, *The Mysore Reversion, an Exceptional Case* (London: Trubner & Co., 1865), 17, accessed 25 April 2014, http://archive.org/stream/mysorereversion00bellgoog/mysorereversion00bellgoog_djvu.txt.

6. C. Hayavadana Rao, *The Mysore Gazetter, Vol. II* (1930): 2883, accessed 25 April 2014, http://archive.org/stream/mysoregazetteerv035381mbp/mysoregazetteerv035381mbp_djvu.txt.

7. Evans Bell, *The Mysore Reversion, an Exceptional Case* (London: Trubner & Co., 1865), 22, accessed 25 April 2014, http://archive.org/stream/mysorereversion00bellgoog/mysorereversion00bellgoog_djvu.txt, accessed 25 April 2014.

8. British Library, India Office Select Materials, accessed 25 April 2014, http://www.bl.uk/catalogues/indiaofficeselect/PhotoEnqFull.asp?PrintID=103056.

9. C. Hayavadana Rao, *The Mysore Gazetter Vol. II* (1930): 2933, accessed 27 April 2014, http://archive.org/stream/mysoregazetteerv035381mbp/mysoregazetteerv035381mbp_djvu.txt.

10. Ibid, v.
11. Ibid, viii.
12. Archaeological Survey of India, History, http://asi.nic.in/asi_aboutus_history.asp, accessed 30 September 2013.
13. Archaeological Survey of India, History, http://asi.nic.in/asi_aboutus_history.asp, accessed 22 September 2013.
14. John Cumming, *Revealing India's Past* (London: The India Society, 1939), 2, accessed 20 September 2013, http://books.google.co.in/books?id=ThGYjlqVe3kC&pg.
15. Alexander Cunningham, *The Ancient Geography of India* (London: Trübner & Co., 1871), xiv, accessed 20 November 2013, http://archive.org/stream/cu31924023029485/cu31924023029485_djvu.txt.
16. Asante Traditional Buildings, UNESCO World Heritage Centre, accessed 3 September 2013, http://whc.unesco.org/pg.cfm?cid=31&id_site=1056.
17. V.N. Prabhakar (lecture delivered at the India International Centre, New Delhi), 'Harappans and their Mesopotamian Contacts', accessed 02 April 2014, http://www.iicdelhi.nic.in/publications/uploads_diary_files/145615June132013_IIC_48_13_06_2013.pdf.

Websites referred:

http://en.wikipedia.org/wiki/Allan_Cunningham_(author), accessed 20 November 2013.

http://en.wikipedia.org/wiki/Alexander_Cunningham, accessed 20 November 2013.

http://en.wikipedia.org/wiki/Joseph_Davey_Cunningham, accessed 2 April 2014.

http://www.britannica.com/EBchecked/topic/146594/Sir-Alexander-Cunningham, accessed 20 November 2013.

http://asi.nic.in/asi_aboutus_history.asp, accessed 20 November 2013.

http://en.wikisource.org/wiki/Cunningham,_Alexander_(1814-1893)_(DNB01), accessed 20 November 2013.

http://bangalorebuzz.blogspot.in/2006/09/street-smart-cunningham-road.html, accessed 3 April 2013.

http://en.wikisource.org/wiki/Cunningham,_Joseph_Davey_(DNB00), accessed 3 April 2013.

http://en.wikipedia.org/wiki/Francis_Cunningham_(Indian_Army_officer), accessed 14 April 2013.

http://newindianexpress.com/cities/bangalore/article1366759.ece, accessed 3 April 2013.

http://asi.nic.in/asi_aboutus_history.asp, accessed 20 November 2013.

Image credits:

Figure 1: Digitized copy of *The Bhilsa Topes* from Google Books, sourced from the Harvard University Library, accessed 24 July 2014, http://books.google.co.in/books?id=r_gWAAAAYAAJ&source=gbs_navlinks_s.

CHAPTER 9

1. Editorials, *Journal of American Medical Association, 188(2)* (April 1964): 174.
2. J.A. Sinton, 'What Malaria Costs India', *Malaria Bureau* 13 (Delhi: Govt of India Press, 1935), 26.
3. Beatrice Potter Webb, *My Apprenticeship* (Cambridge: Press Syndicate of the University of Cambridge, 1979), 258.
4. Ronald Ross, *Memoirs: With a Full Account of the Great Malaria Problem and Its Solution* (London: John Murray, 1923), 96.
5. Ibid, 153-54.
6. Ibid, 189.
7. Ibid, 218.
8. Ibid.
9. Ibid, 221.
10. Ibid, 226.
11. Ibid, 270.
12. Ibid, 318.
13. Leon J. Warshaw, *Malaria: The Biography of a Killer* (New York: Rinehart, 1949), 97.
14. John Carey, ed., *Eyewitness to Science* (Boston: Harvard University Press, 1997), 204.

Websites referred:

http://en.wikipedia.org/wiki/Ronald_Ross, accessed 7 January 2012

http://www.nobelprize.org/nobel_prizes/medicine/laureates/1902/ross-facts.html, accessed 7 January 2012

http://www.nobelprize.org/nobel_prizes/medicine/laureates/1902/ross-bio.
html, accessed 14 January 2012

http://www.britannica.com/EBchecked/topic/510100/Sir-Ronald-Ross,
accessed 3 February 2012

http://www.malariasite.com/malaria/ross.htm, accessed 9 January 2012

http://www.banglapedia.org/HT/R_0220.HTM, accessed 3 February 2012

http://www.poemhunter.com/sir-ronald-ross/biography/, accessed 3
February 2012

http://www.tribuneindia.com/1999/99apr17/saturday/fact.htm, accessed
4 June 2013

http://www.cdc.gov/malaria/about/history/ross.html, accessed 4 June 2013

http://www.answers.com/topic/ronald-ross, accessed 4 June 2013

http://www.medicinae.org/e13, accessed 8 June 2013

https://www.google.com/search?client=gmail&rls=gm&q=manaskhand#q
=19th+Century+Almora&rls=gm, accessed 17 August 2013

http://www.oldindianphotos.in/2011/02/leper-asylum-almora-
uttarakhand-1880s.html, accessed 17 August 2013

http://www.osmania.ac.in/srrip/about_ross.htm, accessed 19 August 2013

http://jmb.sagepub.com/content/17/2/120.extract, accessed, 22 September
2013

http://books.google.co.in/books?id=LGMqAAAAYAAJ&pg=PA878&dq
=Alfred+Bradley+Bloxam&hl=en&sa=X&ei=FimjUq-, accessed 22
September 2013

Image credits:

Figure 1: James Kennedy, *Life and Work in Benares and Kumaon* (New York: Cassel and Company, 1885), accessed 12 April 2014, http://www.gutenberg.org/files/24416/24416-h/24416-h.htm#LEPER.

Figure 2: With kind permission of the Library & Archives Service, London School of Hygiene & Tropical Medicine, accessed 12 July 2014, http://www.cdc.gov/malaria/about/history/ross.html.

CHAPTER 10

1. 'Why Mark Tully needs a Calcutta birth certificate at 78', BBC News, 20 August 2013, accessed 12 November 2013, http://www.bbc.co.uk/news/world-asia-india-23678823.

2. Mark Tully, *Heart of India* (New Delhi: Penguin Books India, 1995), vii.
3. http://digital.library.unt.edu/ark:/67531/metadc4313/m2/1/high_res_d/thesis.pdf, accessed 12 November 2013.
4. Mark Tully, 'My Father's Raj', *Granta*, 57 (Spring 1997): 144-45.
5. BBC News (World edition), accessed 16 December 2013, http://news.bbc.co.uk/2/hi/uk_news/1735083.stm.
6. Mark Tully, *No Full Stops in India* (New Delhi: Penguin Books India, 1988), 4.
7. Peter Victor, 'Tully quits BBC', *Independent*, 10 July 1994, accessed 12 December 2013, http://www.independent.co.uk/news/tully-quits-bbc-1412865.html.
8. BBC News (World edition), accessed 16 December 2013, http://news.bbc.co.uk/2/hi/uk_news/1735083.stm.
9. Book review of *The Defeat of a Congressman and Other Parables of Modern India* by Mark Tully, Foreign Affairs, accessed 16 November 2013, http://www.foreignaffairs.com/articles/47952/donald-s-zagoria/the-defeat-of-a-congressman-and-other-parables-of-modern-india.
10. Donald S. Zagoria, book review of *The Defeat of a Congressman and Other Parables of Modern India* by Mark Tully, Foreign Affairs, Summer 1992 Issue, accessed 10 November 2014, https://www.foreignaffairs.com/reviews/capsule-review/1992-06-01/defeat-congressman-and-other-parables-modern-india
11. Michael Holland, book review of *India in Slow Motion* by Mark Tully, *Observer*, 7 December 2003, accessed 12 February 2015, http://www.theguardian.com/books/2003/dec/07/features.review?INTCMP=SRCH.
12. Bob Drogin, 'Profile: The BBC's Battered Sahib', *Los Angeles Times*, accessed 21 December 2013, http://articles.latimes.com/1992-12-22/news/wr-2472_1_mark-tully.
13. http://blogs.hindustantimes.com/expat-on-the-edge/2010/03/31/i-have-no-plans-to-leave-india-it-is-my-destiny-to-be-here%E2%80%9D-says-sir-mark-tully/, accessed 12 February 2015.
14. Bishakha De Sarkar, 'I would love to be an Indian citizen', *Telegraph*, 20 November 2011.
15. Subhro Niyogi and Saikat Ray, 'Link with India goes back a long way', *Times of India*, 27 November 2013, http://articles.timesofindia.indiatimes.com/2013-11-27/kolkata/44519069_1_mark-tully-india-kolkata.

Websites referred:

http://blogs.hindustantimes.com/expat-on-the-edge/2010/03/31/i-have-no-
plans-to-leave-india-it-is-my-destiny-to-be-here%E2%80%9D-says-
sir-mark-tully/, accessed 18 February 2015.
http://www.telegraphindia.com/1111120/jsp/7days/story_14774725.jsp,
accessed 22 February 2015.
BBC News (World edition): http://news.bbc.co.uk/2/hi/uk_news/1735083.
stm, accessed 22 February 2015.

Image credits:

Figure 1: With kind permission of Sir Mark Tully.

Acknowledgements

In writing my share of the chapters, as always, my best friend and wife Meena did much of the difficult work, editing versions after versions. I can never thank her enough. I am also thankful to my good friend of long standing, Dr Shweta Parikh, whose encouraging comments on an early draft of the work were a big morale booster. And then there are five individuals who have been an integral part of our lives over the years. They are Saroj, Kausalya, Sita, Srinivas and Nizam – who always went beyond their call of duty. I remain eternally grateful to them.

Co-authoring a book can often be a challenging experience, and more so if the co-authors are relative strangers. But Veena turned out to be pleasantly different! Interacting with her was sheer pleasure, and so I owe her a big thanks too.

–Raghu

Many thanks to my co-author Dr Raghunathan for trusting me to be a part of this work, and for his constant encouragement and kind words that enabled me to shed my initial stiffness and write in the sort of pleasantly engaging style he is so well known for.

If my attempts to tell these stories make for enjoyable reading, then credit must go to my dear friend Rohini Pisupati

223

for proofreading early drafts and giving exceptionally pertinent suggestions. Affectionate thanks to my talented niece, Ms Vishakha Ramamurthy, who created the beautiful sketches that appear at the beginning of every chapter.

Much gratitude to my husband Manjunath Gundi and son Amogh for going about the tricky business of living with a writer and making it look easy.

–Veena

Special mention must be made of the generosity of many who took the trouble to source pictures for us and those who granted permission to use images from their collections. While a detailed list of sources can be found at the end of this volume, we would like to individually thank Mr Pradeep Singh, Ms Jessica Davies, Mr V. Narayan Swami, Ms Sarah Walpole, Mr Dokka Srinivasu, Mr David Davies, Mr Vijai Shukul, Mr T. Malcolm Sandilands, Mr Raja Chandra, Mr Laurence Worms, Ms Claire Frankland, Ms Erica Chambers, Ms Joan Ritcey, Ms Iris Kapil, Ms Eisha Neely, Ms Piyal Kundu, Mr S. Thyagarajan, Mr Ashish Kuvelkar, Mr Harsh Vardhan, Prof. Manabendu Banerjee, Dr Frances Pritchett, Mr Rajendra B. Aklekar, and Sir Mark Tully – for making our work so much easier.

And, of course, we are both extremely grateful to the Editor-in-Chief and Publisher at HarperCollins India, Mr Krishan Chopra, whose suggestions on the earlier drafts of the manuscript helped improve the book significantly. We are equally thankful to the copy editor, Mr Siddhesh Inamdar, who with his incisive editing took the level of writing several notches higher.

–Authors